W9-BRM-960

Screenplay Library
Edited by Matthew J. Bruccoli

Irwin R. Blacker, *Consulting Editor*

THE NAKED CITY

A Screenplay
By Malvin Wald
and Albert Maltz

Story by Malvin Wald

Edited by **Matthew J. Bruccoli**
Afterword **by Malvin Wald**

Southern Illinois University Press
Carbondale and Edwardsville

Feffer & Simons, Inc.
London and Amsterdam

Library of Congress Cataloging in Publication Data

Maltz, Albert, 1908–
  The naked city.

  (Screenplay library)
  I. Wald, Malvin, joint author. II. Bruccoli,
Matthew Joseph, 1931–   III. The naked city.
[Motion picture] IV. Series.
PN1997.N324   812'.5'2   79–10826
ISBN 0-8093-0909-2
ISBN 0-8093-0910-6 pbk.
Copyright © 1948 by Gladys Glad Hellinger, and Bank of America,
Martin Gang, and Gladys Glad Hellinger Trustees under the will of Mark J. Hellinger
Published by special arrangement with Gladys Glad Hellinger and
the Trustees of the Mark Hellinger Trust
Afterword by Malvin Wald Copyright © 1979 by Southern Illinois University Press
All rights reserved
Printed in the United States of America
Designed by Gary Gore

Contents

Acknowledgments

The editor acknowledges the generous assistance of Mrs. Hermione K. Brown of Gang, Tyre, and Brown who arranged the publishing of the screenplay by Southern Illinois University Press; and to Mrs. Ben Hamilton of Hampton Books who provided the illustrations for this volume.

The Naked City

Screenplay

by

Malvin Wald

and

Albert Maltz

From a Story

by

Malvin Wald

May 20, 1947

Credits

Screenplay by Malvin Wald and Albert Maltz, from a story by Malvin Wald. Directed by Jules Dassin. Produced by Mark Hellinger for Hellinger Productions and released by Universal-International Pictures.

Lt. Dan Muldoon	Barry Fitzgerald
Frank Niles	Howard Duff
Ruth Morrison	Dorothy Hart
Jimmy Halloran	Don Taylor
Garzah	Ted De Corsia
Dr. Stoneman	House Jameson
Mrs. Halloran	Anne Sargent
Mrs. Batory	Adelaide Klein
Mr. Batory	Grover Burgess
Detective Perelli	Tom Pedi
Mrs. Hylton	Enid Markey
Captain Donahue	Frank Conroy

In the movie Dan Mulvey became Dan Muldoon; Robert Niles became Frank Niles; and Ruth Young became Ruth Morrison. The spelling of Garza was changed to Garzah.

The Naked City

FADE IN

EXT   LONG SHOT OF LOWER
MANHATTAN   A MOONLIT
NIGHT

NARRATOR:
  (an easy, conversational tone)
A city has many faces—

EXT   MIDTOWN MANHATTAN
NIGHT

It's one o'clock in the morning
now—

EXT   WALL STREET   NIGHT
DESERTED

And this is the face of New York
City—

EXT   STATUE OF PROMETHEUS
IN THE CENTER OF THE RA-
DIO CITY BUILDINGS   NIGHT
The fountain beneath the statue
bubbles quietly.

—when it's asleep—

—on a hot summer night—

INT   THE MAIN FLOOR OF A
LARGE BANK   NIGHT
DESERTED

Does money ever sleep, I
wonder?

INT   A LARGE CLOTHING FAC-
TORY   NIGHT
Night lights cast shadows over
the silent machines.

Does a machine become tired?

INT   STAGE OF THE METRO-
POLITAN OPERA   NIGHT
Scenery on the empty stage is lit
by a few night lights.

Or a song?

EXT   EMPIRE STATE BUILDING
NIGHT
We see the flat, monumental sur-
face of stone rising to the sky.

Does stone ever feel weariness?

INT   A MODEST APARTMENT
BEDROOM   NIGHT
Windows open, a fan humming.
A man lies asleep, face down,
sprawled out; his hair is tou-
seled, his pajama top open and
twisted, the sheet thrown back.

MAN'S VOICE
   (wearily)
Some people think it's easy to be
a bank teller. Oh brother!

EXT   AN EAST-SIDE TENEMENT
FIRE ESCAPE   NIGHT   A HUS-
BAND AND WIFE ARE SLEEP-
ING ON BED CLOTHES ON THE
FIRE ESCAPE.

MAN'S VOICE
   (reflectively)
I wonder how many stitches in a
dress? I'll have to count 'em
sometime.

There is a SOUND: of a cater-
wauling cat.

WOMAN'S VOICE
   (amused)
I wonder how many meals I've
cooked in my life? And how
many dishes I've washed?

The woman turns over. CAMERA
HOLDS on sleeping couple.

CAMERA PANS DOWN TO:

EXT   CAT   NIGHT
digging into an open garbage
pail. Nearby another cat sits
patiently.

NARRATOR:
A city asleep—

EXT   THE SKY   NIGHT
We see the silhouette of a plane
with its lights winking for a
landing.

—or as nearly asleep—

EXT   THE CITY AS SEEN FROM
THE PLANE   NIGHT
We see the outline of the bor-
oughs, the lighted bridges that
link them, the lighted arteries
and veins, the upthrust fingers
of stone.

—as any city ever is.

EXT   SINGLE ELEVATED TRAIN
MOVING SLOWLY ON ITS
TRACKS   NIGHT

The pulse of a city like the pulse
of a man—

SOUND: Train wheels.

EXT TUGBOAT ON THE HUDSON TOWING TWO BARGES LOADED WITH FREIGHT NIGHT

SOUND: Boat whistle.

INT ATTENDANT IN AN ELECTRIC CO. SUB STATION NIGHT

SOUND: Hum of dynamos.

INT A DISC JOCKEY PUTTING A RECORD ON A TURNTABLE IN A RADIO STATION.

SOUND: A hot jive recording that blends into the click of linotype keys.

INT A LINOTYPE OPERATOR AT HIS MACHINE IN A NEWSPAPER PRESS ROOM NIGHT

INT A CLEANING WOMAN VACUUMING A CARPET IN THE LOBBY OF THE RADIO CITY MUSIC HALL NIGHT

SOUND: Low hum of the vacuum cleaner.

INT A DRUNKEN, UNSHAVEN BUM IS WATCHING A WINDOW DRESSER IN A SMART FIFTH AVENUE DRESS SHOP. NIGHT THE DRESSER IS HAVING DIFFICULTY IN PULLING A GIRDLE DOWN OVER THE LENGTH OF A DUMMY FIGURE. A SIGN OVER THE SHOP READS: "MADGE LIVINGSTON."

NARRATOR (Cont.)
—can be felt in sleep, slow and steady—

For some men earn their bread at night.

JOCKEY'S VOICE
   (fast)
It starts hot and it ends gutty. Let's go.

OPERATOR'S VOICE
Wonder what the ol' lady made me for lunch tonight? If it's liverwurst again she's got a divorce.

WOMAN'S VOICE
   (wearily, over vacuum sound)
From where I stand this world's made up of nothin' but dirty feet.

BUM'S VOICE
   (Hoarse)
Hey, buddy, do they pay you for that or—(as girdle slips into place over hips) —whoops!

INT WELL-FURNISHED APART-
MENT NIGHT
A group of well-dressed, middle-
aged men and women are playing bridge and drinking. Among
them are Dr. and Mrs. Lawrence
Stoneman.

NARRATOR
And while some people work
and most sleep, others are at the
close of an evening of
relaxation—

SOUND: Rhumba music.

SOUND CONTINUES OVER INTO:

INT NIGHT CLUB NIGHT
Focusing on a ringside table
where a couple—Ruth Young
and Robert Niles—are watching
floor show.

On the bass drum of the orches-
tra are the words: Trinidad Club.

SOUND: Music swells to a more
and more intense beat and then
is suddenly cut off.

INT A WELL-FURNISHED
BEDROOM NIGHT
The only light is from the moon
through the half-raised shade.

NARRATOR
(voice sharp, intense)
And still another — is at the close
of her life.

We dimly perceive an act of
murder: a woman on a bed is
being chloroformed by two men.
She is in a nightgown. One man,
Garza, holds her from behind.
The other, Backalis, holds a
handkerchief over her face. Her
body twists spasmodically,
uselessly.

There is no sound except the
creaking of the bed and the heavy
breathing of the men.

The woman's struggles cease. She slumps back. The men hold her still, the handkerchief over her face. Both men are wearing gloves. We can't see the faces of either man. One of them (Backalis) is wearing a distinctive jacket.

The men lift the body.

BACKALIS
(nervous whisper)
Let's go.

GARZA
(angry whisper)
Don't be a fool. This has to be sure. Lift her up.

BACKALIS
(nervously)
Whatcha gonna do?

GARZA
(slight laugh)
It's a hot night. We'll give her a bath.

They carry the woman into the adjoining bathroom. They lower her into tub. CAMERA FOLLOWS A HAND as it turns on the faucet and the water rushes out.

EXT A STREET DAWN

CLOSE SHOT WATER RUSHING OUT
Water is flowing from a spigot on a street-washing machine that is proceeding slowly down a street in the East Sixties. First faint morning light.

NARRATOR
(quietly)
A hot night working its way toward dawn. And everything is as usual—

Jersey lettuce for New York markets—

EXT A TRUCK LADEN WITH GREEN VEGETABLES EMERGING FROM THE HOLLAND TUNNEL DAWN

EXT WEST WASHINGTON POULTRY MARKET DAWN
A chicken escapes from a crate and a man runs after it.

Tonight's fricassee is somewhat reluctant—

INT   FIRE HOUSE   DAWN

CAMERA is shooting from open doorway at interior. A man at desk, the fire trucks, a sleeping dalmatian dog.

Everything as usual—

EXT   EAST SIDE PIER IN SHADOWS   DAWN
Two men are walking to edge of pier.

—and even this, too, can be called routine in a city of eight million people—

CLOSE SHOT   BACKALIS AND GARZA
Backalis, holding a bottle of whiskey, is drunk. Garza watches him carefully. Both men are in shadows. As Backalis talks, he sits down on edge of pier and looks out over water. He turns so that we see his face. We don't see Garza's face in entire scene.

BACKALIS
(drunkenly—tragically)
I done a lot of things but I never killed nobody . . . Gonna stay drunk for a long time . . . Don't know what I'm gonna say to God when my time comes. He's got a big heart, I'm told, but He don't like—

Backalis never finishes. Garza swings his fist from behind and hits Backalis a blow behind the ear. There is a dull thud as Backalis topples over, his head striking the pier. Garza kneels, pulls the bottle of whiskey out of his hand.

GARZA
(angrily)
I thought you were off the liquor? (angrily—during action) Liquor is bad. Weakens your character—fuzzes your brain—turns you soft. How can a man like me trust a liar like you?

Garza angrily throws the whiskey bottle over the pier. We HEAR a splash. Quickly he thrusts his hand into Backalis's pocket, takes out a chamois bag, puts it in his own. He removes

I can't!

Backalis's wallet, tosses it over.
He looks around swiftly, then lifts
Backalis with his powerful arms.

Garza heaves Backalis over edge
of pier. A low splash. Garza rises,
spits angrily into water, starts off.

EXT THE SKY DAWN IT IS
STREAKED BY MORNING
LIGHT.

NARRATOR
  (softly)
How many things this sky has
seen—

EXT SKY OVER MIDTOWN
DAWN BUILDINGS IN SHOT.
SKY IS GROWING LIGHT.

  (softly)
—that man has done to man.

DISSOLVE TO:

EXT SKY DAY

And now it's morning.

INT BEDROOM DAY
A baby in a crib is howling.
Mother enters shot, putting on
robe. Lifts baby. Smiles fondly,
looking at it as it yowls.

She kisses baby.

MOTHER'S VOICE
Some babies are eight o'clock
babies. Some babies are seven
o'clock babies. Why do you have
to be a six o'clock baby?

EXT THE BOWERY DAY
A drunk is sleeping in a doorway. The sunlight streams down
through the elevated tracks onto
his face. He stirs and blinks—
and turns over for another
snooze.

SOUND: Early Morning
Traffic

NARRATOR
We wake up variously—

—each to his taste.

EXT TENEMENT FIRE ESCAPE
WE SAW EARLIER DAY
An alarm on window sill goes
off. Woman and man awaken.
Man shuts off alarm, leans on el-
bow, yawns . . .

INT KITCHEN OF SMALL
HOUSE DAY
An Italian family. A father and
two grown sons are eating
breakfast. The mother is making
sandwiches for three lunch pails
that stand with tops open.

NARRATOR
  (conversationally)
We've washed and we've shaven
and it's breakfast time.

INT A MASTER DINING ROOM
IN A FIFTH AVENUE MANSION
DAY
An old man, looking very un-
happy, sits at one end of a long,
bare table, staring at a glass of
milk. A butler hovers near him.

OLD MAN'S VOICE
  (in complaint)
Milk! Isn't there anything else for
ulcers except milk?

INT MODEST KITCHEN DAY
Mulvey is making breakfast. He
has a toaster going. On stove two
eggs are boiling. He is watching
a three-minute sand glass that
will tell him when the eggs are
ready. He goes to front door, still
humming, opens it, reaches
down for a bottle of coffee cream.
He returns, pours coffee. Puts
cream in it.

MULVEY
(singing and humming lightly)
After the ball was over,
After the ball was done,
da-da-da-da-, da-da-da . . .
(continues)

CLOSE SHOT COFFEE
Cream is sour. It curdles.

MULVEY
He stops humming, makes a
face. He pours coffee in sink.
Starts to hum again as he takes
eggs off.

EXT TIMES SQUARE ORANGE
DRINK STAND DAY
A customer, eye on wrist watch,
gulping coffee, runs.

NARRATOR
And it's time to go to work.

EXT HALLORAN, WIFE AND FOUR-YEAR-OLD BOY ON FRONT
STEPS OF A TWO-FAMILY HOUSE IN QUEENS DAY

HALLORAN
(straight-faced)
Goodbye, Mrs. Halloran.

MRS. HALLORAN
Goodbye, Mr. Halloran.
(They shake hands, then kiss. Halloran ruffles boy's
hair.)

HALLORAN
(mock rough)
See you tonight, Mac.

BOY
(imitating him)
So long, bud.
Halloran goes off with a smile and a wave.

EXT SUBWAY ENTRANCE DAY
People walking down.

MAN'S VOICE
Gonna be a scorcher today.

GIRL'S VOICE
(nasal)
If it's as bad as yesterday, I'll die, I'll be prostrate.

INT SUBWAY STATION DAY
People crowding platform.

SOUND: Approaching train.

FIRST GIRL'S VOICE
I went to Jones Beach last night. Had a picnic.

SECOND GIRL'S VOICE
With the boy friend?

FIRST GIRL'S VOICE
(dreamily)
Yeah.

SECOND GIRL'S VOICE
Did he get fresh again?

FIRST GIRL'S VOICE
(dreamily)
Yeah.

SECOND GIRL'S VOICE
Gee—you was born with a silver spoon.

EXT AN APARTMENT HOUSE DAY
A woman nods to a doorman as she enters an apartment house.

NARRATOR
For this woman, the day will not be ordinary—

INT FOYER OF APARTMENT HOUSE DAY

Martha Swenson, forty-two years old, a widow—

CAMERA FOLLOWS woman to
elevator. She rings elevator bell.
Door opens. She enters.

INT HALLWAY DAY   —lives a quiet life as a house
Elevator opens. Martha comes   worker—
out, crosses to apartment oppo-
site, opens door.

INT JEAN DEXTER'S APARTMENT DAY

CAMERA is shooting from Martha's POV as she enters living room.
The blinds are drawn so that the light is dim. Martha hesitates at
doorway, then enters quietly. The room is attractively furnished. Martha puts her purse down, crosses to bedroom door, listens. She knocks
softly, knocks again. She opens door, peeks in. Bedroom is dark,
blinds drawn. She sees that bed is unoccupied. She goes in.

                         MARTHA
          Miss Dexter?

She crosses to blind and then notices an overturned, smashed lamp.
As she crosses to it we hear a SOUND from open bathroom door of
water dropping from a tap that has not been completely shut. Martha
looks toward bathtub. With her, we see that the tub is almost ready to
overflow.

CLOSE SHOT ON MARTHA'S FACE
as she walks into bathroom. Her face is suddenly convulsed by horror. Her mouth opens in a soundless scream. Then she turns and
runs.

                         MARTHA
                  (shouting)
          Help me . . . Someone help me . . .

EXT NEW YORK CITY POLICE HEADQUARTERS ON CENTRE
STREET DAY

INSERT SIGN READING:

                    POLICE HEADQUARTERS

                    TELEGRAPH BUREAU

SOUND in BG: A mixture of clicking teletype machines and voices
of telephone operators.

INT   PANEL OF HUGE TELEPHONE SWITCHBOARDS   DAY
A ROW OF FAST-WORKING WOMEN OPERATORS ARE AT THE
SWITCHBOARD.

CAMERA MOVES IN to CLOSEUP of a WOMAN OPERATOR as she
takes a call.

> OPERATOR
> (writing on pad)
> Yes, sir. What's your name, please? . . . Thank you.
> (reaches for telephone plug)

INSERT   TELEPHONE PLUG
being inserted into board under label:

> POLYCLINIC HOSPITAL

EXT   POLYCLINIC HOSPITAL   DAY
as ambulance starts into street.

INT   WOMAN TELEPHONE OPERATOR   DAY

> OPERATOR
> (into mouthpiece)
> One-nine-eight West Six-nine Street. Apartment 4-D.

INT   RADIO ROOM   DAY
A shirt-sleeved patrolman is speaking into a telephone.

> FIRST PATROLMAN
> (into phone)
> Apartment 4-D. Got it.

He writes on a slip of paper, gets up, and walks over to a series of
tables.

INT   PATROLMEN AT PLOTTING TABLES   DAY
These plotting tables have sectional maps of Manhattan on top. On
the maps are little round numbered metallic discs indicating location
of police patrol cars.

INT   PATROLMEN   DAY

> FIRST PATROLMAN
> (handing paper to man at table)
> 20th Precinct. What's out?

INSERT   SECTION OF TABLE-TOP MAP SHOWING TWO METALLIC
DISCS NUMBERED 206 AND 159

                    SECOND PATROLMAN'S VOICE
            Two-oh-six and one-five-nine.

INT TWO PATROLMEN DAY
First patrolman writes on a slip of paper, and brings it over to a radio operator at a microphone. The operator glances at the paper.

INT RADIO OPERATOR AT MICROPHONE DAY
The call letters on the microphone are W-E-P-G.

                        OPERATOR
                    (into microphone)
                Cars two-oh-six—and one-five-nine—
                Cars two-oh-six—and one-five-nine—
                Proceed to one-nine-eight-West—

INSERT TELEPHONE OPERATOR
plugging in another call.

INSERT LABEL ON POLICE SWITCHBOARD READING:

                    MEDICAL EXAMINER

INT AUTOPSY ROOM AT MORGUE DAY
The medical examiner, Dr. Simeon Hoffman, is a paunchy, grey-haired man wearing a surgeon's gown. He is speaking into phone. He puts down phone and starts to write a note.

INSERT POLICE SWITCHBOARD LABEL MARKED:

                    TECHNICAL RESEARCH
                    LABORATORY

as plug is inserted.

INT TECHNICAL RESEARCH LABORATORY DAY LAB TABLES
AND MICROSCOPES ARE EVIDENT IN BG
NICK, a dark-haired man of thirty-five, puts down phone. He takes a puff on a lighted cigarette, writes on a pad, rips off the sheet of paper, and starts to assemble equipment.

INSERT POLICE DEPARTMENT SWITCHBOARD LABEL READING:

                    MANHATTAN HOMICIDE SQUAD

EXT 10TH PRECINCT STATION HOUSE—230 W. 20TH STREET

INT STATION HOUSE DAY
showing sergeant at desk and a few uniformed patrolmen nearby.

CAMERA MOVES UP to a sign near a stairway. Sign reads:

MANHATTAN HOMICIDE SQUAD

THIRD FLOOR

INT   THIRD FLOOR CORRIDOR   DAY
A sign on a door reads:
CAPTAIN SAM DONAHUE
LIEUTENANT DANIEL MULVEY
DISSOLVE THROUGH TO:

INT   DONAHUE'S OFFICE   DAY
CAPTAIN SAM DONAHUE is at his desk, looking at a folder. He
is a husky man of sixty with a wide, pleasant smile and an in-
telligent face. Seated in a chair nearby is Lieutenant Dan Mulvey,
whom we saw, earlier, at breakfast. He is a short, middle-aged
man, who might pass for a bookkeeper. His speech contains a bit
of Irish and a lot of Brooklyn. He is smoking a pipe. He has a
second folder in his lap.

There is nothing in the manner, dress or speech of either man to
suggest the accepted notion of policeman or detective.

DONAHUE
(looking up from folder)
I don't understand this boy Del Vecchio.

MULVEY
(slowly)
I do, Sam . . . I think.

DONAHUE
Do you make any sense out of what he did?

MULVEY
No—but I see eighteen years of feeling lonely and beaten.
So he—
(gestures)
exploded.

DONAHUE
(thoughtfully)
Maybe . . . Sometimes I wonder what the human heart's
made out of.

MULVEY

My wife, rest her soul, always said she'd rather look into a man's heart than into his head—that you could tell more about him.

Donahue turns as BEN MILLER, a chunky police stenographer in plain clothes, enters. He hands a slip of paper to Donahue.

MILLER

This just came in, Captain.
(to Mulvey, as he goes out)
Morning, Lieutenant.

MULVEY

Morning, Ben.

DONAHUE

(reading paper)
You're free, aren't you, Dan?

MULVEY

I haven't had a hard day's work since yesterday.

DONAHUE

(handing him paper)
Woman drowned in a bathtub. Your assignment.

Mulvey nods, gets up, looking at paper.

MULVEY

Who's to do my leg work?

DONAHUE

How about young Halloran again?

MULVEY

(going toward door)
All right. I like the boy.

DONAHUE

How's he doing?

MULVEY

He's makin' the same mistakes I made at his age.

DONAHUE

Too bad. I thought he showed promise.

Mulvey reacts, goes out.

INT   MANHATTAN HOMICIDE SQUAD OFFICE   DAY
A large office with several desks and chairs behind a wooden railing.
Through an open door can be seen some of the cots of the dormitory
where men on night duty sleep. On a bench talking to Ben Miller is
Detective James Halloran, the tall, pleasant-looking young man whom
we saw saying good-bye earlier to his wife. Mulvey takes his hat off
a hat rack. He comes up behind the bench and pauses a foot away to
listen to Halloran, who is talking seriously, with great interest in what
he's saying.

> HALLORAN
> —but that's the point, Ben. In the first six months of a baby's
> life, the father can't get to know it unless he takes care of it
> physically. The idea is to do things for the kid—like bathing
> it.

> MILLER
> But I'm scared to bathe mine. Looks like it'll break.

> HALLORAN
> Then learn how to change it. Is it a bottle baby?

> MILLER
> (boastfully)
> Not mine, he's . . .

> MULVEY
> Begging your pardon—is this the Board of Directors of the
> Diaper Institute?

> HALLORAN
> (rising)
> Hi, Dan.

> MULVEY
> We're on a case, you baby experts.

> HALLORAN
> (eagerly)
> What sort of a case? Something hot?

> MULVEY
> (as they go)
> Dead woman in a bathtub. Something cold.

They go out.

DISSOLVE TO:

EXT   APARTMENT HOUSE ON WEST 69TH STREET   DAY
The ambulance, seen earlier, and two police cars are parked in front.
A small crowd of people is gathered around the entrance. A dark po-
lice sedan drives up. Mulvey, Halloran, Miller step out.

EXT   ENTRANCE TO APARTMENT HOUSE   DAY
CAMERA IS SHOOTING from POV of watching crowd.

> PATROLMAN
> (to Mulvey, with a slight hand salute)
> This way, Lieutenant.

Mulvey, Halloran, and Miller pin their badges on their coat lapels as
they follow the patrolman.

EXT   TO ONE SIDE OF ENTRANCE   MIDDLE-AGED GENTLEMAN,
NURSEMAID, GIRL   DAY
as they look after detectives. The middle-aged gentleman is tall, thin,
shabby, but with pretense to elegance. He carries a walking stick,
wears pince-nez spectacles. The nursemaid is thirtyish, bovine, in
uniform. The girl is five.

> MIDDLE-AGED GENTLEMAN
> (to nursemaid)
> Detectives! You see! I told you it was a murder. I knew!

> LITTLE GIRL
> (pulling nursemaid's hand)
> I wanna go to the park. I wanna see the seals.

> MIDDLE-AGED GENTLEMAN
> (to nursemaid)
> I have the finest crime library in the world . . . with pictures.

> LITTLE GIRL
> (wailing)
> I wanna see the seals.

> NURSEMAID
> (angrily)
> You saw the seals yesterday. This is a murder. It'll educate
> you.

INT   IN FRONT OF JEAN DEXTER'S APARTMENT   DAY
A patrolman at door gives a half salute, admits detectives.

INT   LIVING ROOM   DAY
Two plainclothes detectives are standing in the room. The maid, Martha Swenson, is seated in an easy chair. She is distraught and evidently has been crying. Near her is NED HARVEY, the apartment superintendent, a thin, middle-aged man, wearing work pants and a grey sweater. Throughout scene Miller takes shorthand notes of what is said.

                    MULVEY
          Who's in charge here?
One of the plainclothes detectives steps forward.

                    DETECTIVE
          Me, sir—Detective Sergeant Shaeffer, 20th Precinct.

                    MULVEY
          What's the story?

                    SHAEFFER
                (consulting notebook)
          The dead woman's name is Jean Dexter. Twenty-six years
          old, unmarried. She used to be a dress model at Madge Livingston's, on Fifth Avenue. Her parents live in Lakewood,
          New Jersey. Their name is Batory—that's Polish. Her name
          used to be Mary Batory until she came to New York. The
          ambulance doctor says she died of drowning . . . that's all I
          have.

                    MULVEY
                (to Miller)
          Got it?
Miller nods, scribbling. Puffing on his pipe, Mulvey walks over to an end table and squats down a little to look at a framed photograph without touching it.

INSERT   BEAUTIFUL BLONDE GIRL IN EVENING DRESS

                    MULVEY'S VOICE
          This her?

                    SHAEFFER'S VOICE
          Yeah.

INT   BACK TO SCENE   DAY
Mulvey looks inquiringly at Martha Swenson.

SHAEFFER

Martha Swenson, the woman's housekeeper. She found
the body.
(indicating Harvey)
Mr. Harvey, the house superintendent. He called headquarters.

MULVEY

(nodding)
Where's the body?

SHAEFFER

(pointing)
In there.

Mulvey starts toward bedroom followed by Halloran and Miller.

INT BEDROOM DAY

On the bed is a body covered by a sheet. Standing by the bed is a
uniformed patrolman. A white-coated ambulance doctor is filling out
a paper form. The door to the bathroom is open, with part of the tub
visible.

As Mulvey sees the body on the bed, he stops.

MULVEY

(quiet . . . but angry)
Didn't this woman drown in a bathtub, doctor?

DOCTOR

She was on the bed when I got here.

Mulvey goes toward living room angrily.

INT LIVING ROOM DAY

as Mulvey comes into doorway.

MULVEY

Who moved the body?

MARTHA

(rising; upset)
When I came in and . . . saw her like that in the tub . . . I
called Mr. Harvey, here. He—helped me.

MULVEY
(sharply)
You should've waited for the police! Both of you should
have known better.

MARTHA
(wringing hands)
I was so upset . . .

HALLORAN
(entering)
There's a bottle of pills under the bed, Dan. Looks like
sleeping pills.

MULVEY
(holding out hand)
Let me see 'em.

HALLORAN
(startled)
I left 'em there.

MULVEY
Why, thank you for that, Jimmy.
(looks at Martha and Harvey)
This is moving day around here. I thought maybe you caught
the fever.

HALLORAN
About those pills . . . maybe the dame took an overdose?

MULVEY
(patiently)
Jimmy, it's our obligation to wait for the medical examiner.
He's a learned physician employed by the city to determine
the causes of mysterious deaths. Let the good man earn his
money.
Halloran grins with slight embarrassment.

DISSOLVE TO:

INT BEDROOM GROUP (FAVORING DR. HOFFMAN) DAY
Standing by the bed is the medical examiner, whom we saw earlier;
Mulvey, Halloran are with him. Ben Miller is taking notes in the back-
ground. Nick, whom we saw earlier in the Technical Laboratory, is
standing by with his spray equipment for fingerprints.

DR. HOFFMAN

No accident and no suicide. There are bruises on her throat, shoulders and arms. Those slight burns around her mouth and nose were caused by chloroform. She was chloroformed after a struggle, then dumped into the tub alive.

HALLORAN
(eagerly)
How can you tell that, Doctor?

HOFFMAN

By the white foam around her mouth. It's proof she drowned.
(to Mulvey; indicating Halloran)
New?

MULVEY
(nodding)
New.

INT ANOTHER ANGLE THE GROUP DAY
A police photographer has set up his lighting equipment and large 8-by-10 camera.

PHOTOGRAPHER
(to Mulvey)
Okay, Lieutenant?

MULVEY
(to Hoffman)
Okay, Doctor?

DR. HOFFMAN
(putting instruments away)
The body's yours.

MULVEY

Start working, gentlemen.
The room becomes very active. Halloran goes into bathroom. Photographer begins taking flashlight pictures of room, bed, etc. Nick begins to spray a glass on a night table with a colored powder from an atomizer, seeking fingerprints.

Mulvey writes a note, looks at bed, writes another note. Halloran comes out of bathroom with a pair of men's silk pajamas.

>   HALLORAN
>
> Dan . . . these were in the laundry hamper. No laundry
> marks and no label.

Mulvey takes the pajamas, feels the material.

>   MULVEY
>
> Real fancy. You don't get these for three ninety-five.
>   (to Nick)
> Pick up these pajamas on your way out, Nick. I want 'em
> under your X-ray machine.

>   NICK
>
> Right.

Mulvey, followed by Halloran and Miller, goes into living room.

INT   LIVING ROOM   DAY

Martha Swenson and Harvey are seated on a couch as Mulvey, Shaeffer, and Halloran enter the room. Patrolman stands at door. Throughout this scene we get flashes of light from the busy photographer in the bedroom.

>   MULVEY
>
> Who belongs to these?

>   MARTHA
>
> I—I don't know, sir.
>   (wringing hands)
> I'm so unstrung.

>   MULVEY
>
>   (quietly)
> I know you are. But I think you'd like to help us.

>   MARTHA
>
> I would—I would. Such a sweet girl, she was. A little wild,
> by my standards maybe, but live and let live, I say. Always
> treated me swell.

>   MULVEY
>
> The pajamas, Martha.

>   MARTHA
>
> I'm all in pieces. I . . .

Mulvey holds out the pajamas.

MARTHA
(hesitantly)
They could belong to Mr. Henderson.
(wringing hands)
This is awful. I might be getting someone in trouble.

MULVEY
We don't want to get the wrong person in trouble either
. . . What's his first name?

MARTHA
(in a rush)
Philip, I think. He lives in Baltimore. That's what she told
me. I only saw him once or twice. I only know he was an
admirer of Miss Dexter's.

MULVEY
(fingering pajamas)
Seems likely.

MARTHA
Oh, I'm all in little pieces. What a nightmare!

MULVEY
You're being a big help to us, Martha . . . How old would
you say Mr. Henderson is?

MARTHA
Oh . . . fifty about.

MULVEY
What does he look like?

MARTHA
Oh—he's real distinguished, real. About as tall as him.
(points to Halloran)
Got grey hair. And strong-looking for his age. No corpora-
tion on him, if you know what I mean.

MULVEY
Uh-huh.
(to Miller)
Got it?
(Miller nods . . . to Harvey)
Do you know Henderson?

HARVEY

Never saw him.

MULVEY

(to Miller)

Shoot a wire on this to Baltimore.

Miller nods. Hoffman comes into living room, carrying medical case.

HOFFMAN

Here's the ring she was wearing.

(Mulvey takes ring)

I'll phone you after the autopsy . . . Have fun.

MULVEY

(looking at ring)

Likewise.

Hoffman goes out.

MARTHA

(eagerly)

Sir . . . that ring . . . it's a black star sapphire . . . very rare.
She said her brother sent it from India.

MULVEY

Did she have any other jewelry?

MARTHA

Oh—a lot. Valuable. She kept it in a jewel box, locked.

MULVEY

Let's go get it.

(as Martha hesitates)

Please.

Hesitantly Martha goes into bedroom, the others following. At the
moment of their entrance, Nick is spraying the surface of the vanity
table with iodine vapor. The photographer, lying on his side, is making a photograph of the floor beneath the bed.

PHOTOGRAPHER

(to Nick)

Okay . . . You can pick up that bottle under the bed now.

NICK

(spraying)

Check.

MULVEY

Nick—can we open a drawer in that table?

NICK

Yeah. I've gone over them.

MARTHA

(horrified)

What are you doing to the furniture?

NICK

(smiling)

Investigating it.

During the ensuing scene, Nick puts down the atomizer, crawls under bed and gets the bottle out by means of looping a string over the neck of it.

MULVEY

Come on, Martha.

Martha opens a drawer. A startled look comes to her face. She frantically pulls open the other drawer.

MARTHA

She had bracelets and rings . . . diamond rings . . . They're all gone. It must have been thieves that killed her.

MULVEY

(Softly, to Halloran)

Another detective.

(to Martha)

Could you describe the jewelry?

MARTHA

Most of it, I think.

MULVEY

Fine. Go in and rest yourself now.

As Martha goes out, Nick stands up, holding the bottle of pills by the looped string.

NICK

Looks like Seconal.

MULVEY
(Peering at it)
Jimmy—I want to start questioning those two in there. You start your leg work. Get the number of this prescription, see the druggist. From him go to the doctor. Then go to the dress shop she worked at.

HALLORAN
Right.

He writes down druggist's name and prescription number. The policeman comes to door of living room.

POLICEMAN
Lieutenant—the newspaper men are here.

MULVEY
Okay, I'm coming.
(to Nick)
Getting any fingerprints, Nick?

NICK
Nothing good so far. Half prints, quarter prints—that's all.

MULVEY
(going toward living room . . . soberly—to Halloran)
Looks to me like a heavy case—a heavy case.
DISSOLVE TO:

EXT MADISON AVE. DAY

SOUND: Street noises

Halloran moves to one side to avoid a fat man with an English bulldog on leash. An itinerant bootblack gestures toward his shoes but he shakes his head. He pauses at the entrance to a drugstore on the corner, checks the address against his memo book, goes in.

NARRATOR
(conversationally, heard above street noises)
An investigation for murder is under way now in the city of New York. It will advance methodically, by trial and error, by leg and brain work, by asking a thousand questions to get one answer. Ever look for a needle in a dark house? You can find it—if you're patient enough. Just get down on your knees, examine every inch of every floor of every

INT DRUGSTORE DAY
There is no one at the prescription counter. He rings a little bell placed there for that purpose. The druggist appears, a short, bald, stout man. Halloran shows him his badge in the palm of his hand, speaks to him, reads from his memo book. Druggist disappears for an instant, returns with his prescription book, turns the pages until he finds the Dexter prescription.

room—and you'll find it. The Homicide Squad, my friends, is made up of patient men. Ever work a jigsaw puzzle? Ever try to find a murderer? Ever play button-button?

DRUGGIST AND HALLORAN

DRUGGIST
Dr. Lawrence Stoneman—office in the Squibb Building.
(leans forward)
Confidentially—a doctor in the dough—high class.

HALLORAN
(writing)
Do you happen to remember Miss Dexter?

DRUGGIST
(shaking head)
A one-shot customer.

HALLORAN
Not even by the fact you made up sleeping pills for her?
Druggist laughs, leans forward.

DRUGGIST
Confidentially, half the people in this city can't sleep without pills. Hurry up . . . hurry up . . . too much hurry up.

HALLORAN
Thanks. You've been a help.

As Halloran starts out of drugstore CAMERA FOLLOWS HIM.

NARRATOR
Ask a question, get an answer, write it down . . .

INT DEXTER'S LIVING ROOM DAY
Patrolman at door. Martha Swenson on couch. Mulvey, puffing his
pipe, has memo book in hand. Mulvey has his coat off.

MULVEY
Did she have any other men friends?

MARTHA
None I know of, sir. Just this Niles man. Robert Niles—a
lovely man.

Mulvey scribbles in memo book, rubs his nose thoughtfully, rises,
crosses living room to bedroom door, opens it.

INT BEDROOM DAY
The bedroom lights have been switched off. Nick is operating a portable ultra-violet lamp. It casts a beam of intense violet light. He is
using it like a searchlight to explore every inch of the walls. The bedroom has been transformed since we last saw it—ripped apart. The
bed has been taken down, wallpaper stained in various spots, lamps
taken apart, etc.

MULVEY
(softly)
How are you doing, Nick?

NICK
(softly)
Not too bad. Found two grey hairs on the rug.

MULVEY
Grey, eh? . . . How about fingerprints?

NICK
No good ones yet.

Mulvey closes door, crosses to Martha, looks closely at her hair. Martha draws back in alarm.

MULVEY
(smiling)
Don't you mind me. Just admirin' your hair.

Martha smiles a little, flattered.

DISSOLVE TO:

EXT A STREET DAY
Halloran is wiping his sweaty
face as he walks. He stops, looks
up.

EXT SQUIBB BUILDING DAY
stretching to sky.

EXT AT THE ENTRANCE DAY
Halloran is entering building.

NARRATOR
(leisurely)
Ask a question and take a walk.
Hop a bus and ask a question.
Jimmy Halloran's an expert with
his feet. He pounded a beat in
the Bronx for a year as a cop . . .
during the war he walked half-
way across Europe with a rifle in
his hand.

Ever play button-button in a city
of eight million people—

INT DR. STONEMAN'S RECEPTION ROOM DAY
A medium-sized room, tastefully furnished. Two patients waiting,
both women in their middle years, well dressed. An elderly nurse at
desk. Nurse looks up as Halloran enters. He approaches desk, speaks
quietly.

HALLORAN
Is Dr. Stoneman in?

NURSE
(dubiously)
Do you have an appointment?

HALLORAN
I'm from the Police Department. It's quite important.
(shows his badge)

NURSE
Just a moment.
She goes out of room. Halloran walks to a large window that looks
out over the city.

INT THE CITY FROM HALLORAN'S POV DAY
NARRATOR
There's the layout, Jim. The man
who killed Jean Dexter is
somewhere down there. Can't
blame him for hiding, can you?

NURSE'S VOICE
Dr. Stoneman'll see you.

INT WAITING ROOM DAY
Halloran follows nurse through door into a corridor, then into an office.

INT STONEMAN'S PRIVATE OFFICE DAY
Dr. Stoneman, in a white gown, is just coming through another door from an examination room. He is a handsome, keen-looking man of fifty, with iron-grey hair. We saw him playing bridge at 1:00 A.M.

DR. STONEMAN
Yes sir. What can I do for you? Have a seat.

HALLORAN
(sitting)
I want to ask you about a patient of yours—Jean Dexter.
Stoneman, who has been walking around to his swivel chair, pauses, turns.

DR. STONEMAN
Dexter? Are you sure she's my patient?

HALLORAN
You wrote a prescription for her two weeks ago—Seconal.
Stoneman thinks, then nods.

STONEMAN
Yes, a blonde girl. Very handsome, I remember now . . . Dexter.
(sits; starts going through card file)
What department are you from, Officer?

HALLORAN
Homicide.

STONEMAN
(stiffening)
Oh? Don't tell me that girl murdered someone?

HALLORAN
Someone murdered her.

STONEMAN
What?

(a pause—very distressed)
My goodness . . . when . . .

HALLORAN

Last night sometime.
A pause. Stoneman shakes his head. Pulls card out of file.

STONEMAN

What do you want to know?

HALLORAN

Whatever you can tell me about her.

STONEMAN

(angrily)
She needed a good spanking. Took Benzedrine by day,
needed sleeping pills at night. I told her to slow up—but
no. Life was too short for her.
(shakes head again)

STONEMAN (Cont.)

Burned out now. All her fresh, young beauty on a scrap
heap. Excuse me, Officer, but I'm a doctor because I'm interested in people. I hate to see human beings waste
themselves.
(shrugs, falls silent)

HALLORAN

Can you tell me anything else about her? Her life—her
friends?

STONEMAN

No. Nothing. I only saw her that one visit.

HALLORAN

I guess that's all, Doctor. Thank you.
(stands)
Stoneman nods and tosses the card on the desk. Halloran leaves.

EXT   MADGE LIVINGSTON'S DRESS SHOP ON FIFTH AVENUE
DAY
This is the same shop we saw in the early morning. Two young, shab-
bily dressed girls are staring at a glittering evening dress on dummy
in window.

> FIRST GIRL

Imagine me in that!

> SECOND GIRL

I can't imagine.

> FIRST GIRL

In the Sert Room of the Waldorf Astoria. With Frankie singing.

> SECOND GIRL

I can't imagine.

> FIRST GIRL

Gosh, I'd commit murder for a dress like that. It's a pome by Shakespeare, that's what it is. Lookit that feller. What do you suppose he's buying?

HALLORAN FROM POV OF THE GIRLS   DAY
He is talking to a woman.

> SECOND GIRL'S VOICE

I can't imagine.

> FIRST GIRL'S VOICE

Oh, you—you're so uncooperative I could slam you.

INT   MADGE LIVINGSTON'S DRESS SHOP   DAY
Mrs. Livingston is handsome, middle-aged, well tailored, with a fancy way of speaking.

> MRS. LIVINGSTON
> (seriously)

. . . and somewhere in the back of her pretty head there was a fixed notion that she couldn't be happy without being rich. I don't think Jean ever would have married unless the man had money—real money.

> HALLORAN

Why did you fire her?

> MRS. LIVINGSTON
> (shrugs)

Gentlemen sometimes come here with their wives. When Jean Dexter modeled, many of them left my shop a little too interested in her. Their wives didn't like it—and neither did I.

HALLORAN

I see. Can I talk to her friend now—the model you spoke about?

MRS. LIVINGSTON

(rising)

Ruth Young? Yes. I'll call her.

She leaves.

EXT   AT SHOP WINDOW   DAY

FIRST GIRL

You see—he's gonna buy something. Oh, I can't bear it.

SECOND GIRL

It's getting late. We better go.

FIRST GIRL

So what if we're late?

SECOND GIRL

The boss'll holler.

FIRST GIRL

Let him holler. Strengthen his lungs. Oh, lookit.

EXT   HALLORAN FROM POV OF THE GIRLS   DAY

Madge Livingston and Ruth Young approaching him.

Ruth Young is a lovely girl in her early twenties. She is wearing a striking evening gown. As the two girls talk, we see Mrs. Livingston introduce Halloran and Ruth and leave them.

FIRST GIRL

Oh, I can't bear it. Oh, I'm going. What a dress. It's a pome.

SECOND GIRL

A pome. By you everything's a pome.

FIRST GIRL

(leaving)

Oh, Millie—you got no imagination.

She leaves. Other follows, looking offended.

INT DRESS SHOP DAY
Ruth has a quiet, attractive manner, good speech.

                    HALLORAN
         Miss Young—I understand you modeled with Jean Dexter?

                         RUTH
              (nodding)
         We're friends, too.
              (hesitates)
         Is she in trouble, Mr. Halloran?

                    HALLORAN
         Well. . . . She *is* kind of wild, isn't she?

                         RUTH
         Oh, no . . . Maybe Mrs. Livingston would call her wild, but
         I wouldn't. She's full of fun . . . wonderful company.

                    HALLORAN
         Do you know anybody who has cause to dislike her?

RUTH

No . . .

HALLORAN

How about Mrs. Henderson?

RUTH

Who's she?

HALLORAN

Well, Miss Dexter and *Mr.* Henderson are very friendly, aren't they?

RUTH

She never told me about a man named Henderson.

HALLORAN

(disappointed)
Are you sure?

RUTH

Really, Mr. Halloran—Jean's my friend—I don't think I want to answer any more questions unless you tell me why you're asking them.

HALLORAN

(watching her)
She was found dead this morning.
Ruth gasps. Her face goes white. She looks as though she will collapse. Halloran grabs her arm, pulls a chair up.

HALLORAN

(gently)
Sit down . . . Rest a moment.
(Ruth obeys)
I'm sorry.
Halloran walks over to a water cooler for a glass of water.

NARRATOR
Learn anything, Halloran? How does it add up? Button, button, where's the button?
DISSOLVE TO:

EXT 10TH PRECINCT STATION HOUSE DAY
An elderly fireman has opened a hydrant on this hot summer day for
the neighborhood kids. A half dozen kids in bathing suits, trunks and
underwear shorts are reveling in the water. A boy of ten, lying on the
street, puts his face in the water, blows bubbles.

> BOY
> I'm a whale. Lookit . . .
> (blows bubbles)
> Lookit me . . . I'm a whale.

A tough little girl of twelve sneaks up behind him, pushes his head
under water, runs off. During this, two men have come along street—
Niles and Perelli. Boy gets up, gasping.

> BOY
> I'll moider you. I'll cut your head off.

> FIREMAN
> (reprovingly)
> Such language.

One of the two men—Robert Niles—laughs.

> NILES
> (to fireman—in passing)
> In front of a police station, too.

CAMERA HOLDS on two men going up station steps.

INT MULVEY'S OFFICE DAY
A smaller office than Donahue's. Simply furnished. On Mulvey's desk
there is a photograph of a pleasant-looking woman in her late twenties, with two little girls. They are dressed in the fashion of 1920. Mulvey is at his desk, Miller in a chair. Miller is reading from notebook.

> MILLER
> The janitor's story of his whereabouts last night is being
> checked. Ditto the maid. No report yet on fingerprints. Con-
> stentino is on his way to Lakewood to see the girl's parents.

Door opens. One of the two men we saw on the street a moment
earlier comes in. He is Detective Perelli, forty, husky, hard-faced.

> PERELLI
> Got Robert Niles, Lieutenant.

MULVEY

Have him in.
> (rises, starts cleaning pipe)

NILES enters, a man in his early thirties. He is tall, unusually hand-some, with a straightforward, attractive quality about him. He wears a Service Discharge emblem. Perelli shuts door, sits down in corner.

MULVEY

Thank you for coming down, Mr. Niles. I'm Lieutenant Mulvey.
> (gestures)

Make yourself comfortable. This is Sergeant Miller.

NILES
> (sitting down—smiling)

How do you do . . .
> (looks around)

I've never been in a police station. Why'd you want to see me, Lieutenant?

MULVEY
> (cleaning pipe)

Just a routine check on something. Did you ever run across a girl named . . .
> (looks at paper as though he had forgotten name)

. . . Dexter?

NILES

Jean Dexter? Why, yes . . . we're good friends.

MULVEY

How long have you known her?

NILES

A little over a year. She helps me out in my business occa-sionally. She's a model.

MULVEY

What business is that?

NILES

Merchandising consultant.
> (hands Mulvey a card)

I help out-of-town buyers get woolens, dress goods . . .
Anything in the textile line.

                    MULVEY
Do you pay Miss Dexter a salary?

                    NILES
No . . . just a . . . bonus from time to time when she does
something.

                    MULVEY
Like what?

                    NILES
     (shrugs)
Modeling . . . entertaining somebody for me.

                    MULVEY
When did you see her last?

                    NILES
Yesterday. We had lunch together. Why?

                    MULVEY
You haven't seen her since?

                    NILES
No. Is anything the matter?
     (leans forward)

                    MULVEY
     (softly)
She's dead. Murdered.

Niles sinks back, shocked, incredulous. Mulvey watches him. Perelli
leaves quietly.

INT   OUTER OFFICE OF HOMICIDE SQUAD   DAY
Halloran and Ruth come in. Ruth has changed to street clothes. Halloran motions for her to wait, crosses to a detective at a desk—a man
of fifty-five, HENRY FOWLER.

                    HALLORAN
     (low-voiced)
Mulvey back yet?

FOWLER
Inside. Talking to a guy.
Halloran presses buzzer on desk and picks up phone.

HALLORAN
(into phone—low-voiced)
Dan? Jimmy. Got a girl here—Ruth Young. Friend of Dexter's. Model at Livingston's.

INT MULVEY'S OFFICE DAY

MULVEY
(into phone; writing a memo)
Hold it. I'll buzz.
As Mulvey puts down phone, Niles looks at him, shakes his head.

NILES
This is terrible. I feel sick over it.
Niles raises his hands, looks at them. They are trembling.

                              NILES
                        (continuing)
          My hands haven't trembled like this since I was in the South
          Pacific.

                              MULVEY
                        (conversationally)
          What happened to you there?

                              NILES
                        (tossing it off)
          Oh . . . my first time in combat . . .

                              MULVEY
          What outfit were you in?

                              NILES
          Seventy-seventh . . .

INT CLOSE SHOT OF MILLER DAY
writing down a memo.

                        MULVEY'S VOICE
          I think I had a cousin in that one. It's a New York division,
          isn't it?

                        NILES'S VOICE
          Yes.

INT BACK TO SCENE DAY

                              MULVEY
          Corporal James Dennis . . .

                              NILES
          Don't remember him. I was a Captain.
Mulvey, starting to stuff his pipe, looks across the room at Miller.
Miller rises quietly, goes out.

                              MULVEY
          We want to find the person who murdered Jean Dexter, Mr.
          Niles.

                              NILES
                        (leaning forward—passionately)
          Anything I can tell you!

MULVEY
Anyone you know who might've had a reason to kill her?

NILES
(shaking head)
Everyone liked Jean.

MULVEY
(glancing at memo book)
Do you happen to know a friend of Miss Dexter's called Ruth Young?

NILES
(hesitating)
Ruth Young? No, I . . . Oh, yes . . . a model, isn't she?

MULVEY
I think so. How well do you know her?

NILES
I've met her once or twice at parties Jean gave.
Mulvey presses buzzer twice.

MULVEY
And how long did you know Miss Dexter?

NILES
About a year.

MULVEY
See her often?

NILES
Why, yes, I . . .
The door opens. Halloran appears with Ruth Young. Ruth sees Niles, who has turned.

RUTH
(running to him)
Robert, why are *you* here?

NILES
(awkwardly)
Why, hello, Ruth.
Ruth catches hold of his arm, turns to Mulvey angrily.

RUTH
You don't think *he* could've been involved in Jean's death?
He hardly knew her.

MULVEY
(flatly)
How do *you* know?

RUTH
Well, of course I know! Robert and I are engaged.

MULVEY
Congratulations.
He looks steadily at Niles, who shifts very uneasily.

DISSOLVE TO:

INT TECHNICAL RESEARCH LAB DAY
Nick and an assistant are carefully examining Henderson's pajamas under an X-ray machine.

NARRATOR
The items that make up this murder are being compiled now . . .

INT AUTOPSY ROOM OF THE MORGUE DAY

Dr. Hoffman, in a surgical gown and mask, wipes the perspiration off his forehead. His assistant hands him a surgical instrument.

They'll be listed in a folder marked Dexter, Jean . . . along with some questions . . .

EXT PENNSYLVANIA STATION DAY
as a detective approaches a taxicab dispatcher. The two men exchange a few words, and the dispatcher makes a notation in his notebook.

Is Henderson the murderer? Did a taxicab take him to the Pennsylvania Railroad Station?

INT BALTIMORE POLICE STATION DAY CLOSE SHOT BULLETIN BOARD MARKED: "18TH PRECINCT STATION, BALTIMORE, MD." A HAND REACHES IN, PINS A NOTICE ON BOARD.

NARRATOR
Who is Henderson? Where does he live? Who knows him?

INSERT OF NOTICE READING:
"POLICE CHIEF, BALTIMORE,
MD. PLEASE ASCERTAIN INFO
ABOUT RESIDENT YOUR CITY
NAME PHILIP HENDERSON
AGE ABOUT 50, GREY HAIR,
TALL BUILD. CONFIDENTIAL.
QUICK REPLY URGENT.
        MULVEY, NEW YORK"

CAMERA PULLS BACK to
SHOW several detectives moving
in to read it.

INT   OFFICE BUILDING HALLWAY   DAY
as janitor admits Perelli to office. Sign on door reads:
               ROBERT NILES
          BUSINESS CONSULTANT

INT   NILES'S OFFICE   DAY

                    PERELLI
          (as they enter)
     Do you know Niles?
The janitor smiles smugly, waves his hand. He is a small man, bald.

                    JANITOR
     Sure. I keep tabs on everybody. I'm sharp.

                    PERELLI
     What kind of a business does he run?

                    JANITOR
     He don't run any.
They are looking around the office now. It is sparsely furnished.

                    PERELLI
     How do you know?

                    JANITOR
     I'm sharp. Nobody comes to see him. No secretary. Nothing
     to clean out of his waste basket. Don't spend much time
     here himself. He's a bust.
Perelli goes to desk, opens side drawers. The first one is empty. The
second has a bottle of whiskey. The third has an autographed photo
of Jean Dexter.

                TO SWEETHEART
                FROM JEAN

Perelli closes drawers, tries middle drawer. It is empty except for a book: *The Campaigns of the South Pacific*. Perelli closes drawer, starts out.

                JANITOR
       (smugly)
  See . . . told you I was sharp.

INT   OUTER OFFICE OF HOMICIDE SQUAD   DAY
Mulvey is escorting Ruth Young to the door.

                MULVEY
  I might be wanting to see you again.

                RUTH
  Any time you say.
       (quietly)
  Jean was my friend.

                MULVEY
  You won't leave town without letting me know?
       (opening door)

                RUTH
  Oh? All right . . . Good-bye.

                MULVEY
  'Bye.
       (closes door—turns to Fowler)
  Lovely girl, isn't she? Lovely.

                FOWLER
  Yeah!

                MULVEY
  Lovely long legs.

                FOWLER
  Yeah—yeah.

                MULVEY
  Keep looking at 'em.

                FOWLER
  A pleasure.

Fowler rises, grabs Panama hat, leaves. As Mulvey crosses back to office, Miller holds up his hand to intercept him. Miller is talking on the phone, seated at a desk. He is scribbling a note.

> MILLER
> (into phone)
> Thanks.

He hangs up, rises, speaks to Mulvey.

> MILLER
> Couple of things. One: Medical examiner called in. Dexter died between one and two A.M.

> MULVEY
> I see.

> MILLER
> (handing him memo)
> And here are a few interesting items on our friend inside.

Mulvey reads the memo, exchanges a look with Miller, then goes into his office, followed by Miller.

INT MULVEY'S OFFICE DAY
as Mulvey and Miller enter. Niles is seated, smoking comfortably. Halloran is sitting behind him.

> MULVEY
> (with a smile)
> Mr. Niles . . .

> NILES
> (returning smile—gracefully)
> These things happen, Lieutenant. I told you I didn't know Ruth Young very well. Now you know we're engaged.
> (grins)
> Can't blame a man for wanting to keep his fiancée out of a murder case, can you?

> MULVEY
> (pleasantly)
> I never had a fiancée in a murder case.
> (ingratiatingly)
> And just between ourselves . . . you never told your fiancée what good friends you and Miss Dexter were—did you?

NILES

Ruth's a bit jealous, Lieutenant.
(frankly)
You understand. . . .

MULVEY

Uh huh . . . I wonder now . . . is there anything else you told me that isn't . . . strictly true?

NILES

(earnestly)
I have no reason to lie to you, Lieutenant.

MULVEY

(softly)
I've got a report in front of me says you never were in the South Pacific, Mr. Niles. You weren't in the 77th Division. You weren't an officer. You weren't in the Army.

Niles's smile has faded. He looks wretched.

NILES

(miserably)
I suppose you think I'm a heel . . .
(passionately)
I didn't even wait for the draft. I tried to enlist. They wouldn't take me. I've got a trick knee from college football. I just couldn't get in.

MULVEY

That's all right with me . . . but why lie about it?

NILES

I don't know. Stupid pride, I suppose.

MULVEY

How did you spend the war years, Mr. Niles?

NILES

I was in Chicago. Same business I have now.

MULVEY

Been at it long?

NILES

Six or seven years. Since college.

MULVEY

Doing pretty well?

NILES

Very good these days.

Mulvey picks up phone, buzzes at same time.

MULVEY

(into phone)

Is Perelli back?

(pause)

Send him in.

(pause)

Mulvey smiles at Niles. Niles smiles back. Door opens, Perelli enters.

MULVEY

What can you tell us about Mr. Niles's business?

Niles stiffens.

PERELLI

He ain't got a business. It's a dodge. No credit rating. Dropped from his university club for nonpayment of dues. Still owes a food and liquor bill of $110.83.

A pause. Niles looks very crestfallen.

MULVEY

(genially)

I've been thirty-eight years on the force, Mr. Niles. I've been a cop on the beat, I've been with the Safe and Loft Squad, I've been twenty-two years in the Homicide Division. But in a lifetime of interrogatin' an' investigatin', you are probably the biggest an' most willing liar I ever met.

NILES

(bursting out)

All right, I'm a liar. I'm a circus character altogether. But I didn't kill Jean Dexter. I told you where I was last night. Why don't you check on that?

MULVEY

We're doing that right now.

NILES

(angrily)

Okay then. That's fine.
(suddenly—a change of mood)
I'm sorry. I'm not angry at you, Lieutenant. You're just doing your job. The truth is I'm ashamed of myself.
(frankly)
My family used to have money and position. Since I got out of college, I haven't been much of a success. I'm trying to keep up a front . . .
(earnestly)
But I'm only a small-time liar, Lieutenant. Believe me. On important things I'm straight as a die.

MULVEY
(softly)
Every man to his taste.

NILES
Ask me anything you want. Jean was my friend. I want to help you.

MULVEY
(consulting notebook)
You spent close to fifty dollars last night at the Trinidad Club. Where'd you get the money?
Niles hesitates, then speaks frankly, with obvious shame.

NILES
I play a sharp game of bridge with Park Avenue friends. I take a flier on the stock market. On inside tips. When I'm hard up, I borrow money . . . That's the truth.

MULVEY
Thank you . . .
(consulting notebook)
Now about this man Henderson. You say you only met him once in Miss Dexter's apartment. Would you describe him to me?

NILES
Well . . . medium height; husky; blonde hair; wore glasses . . . looked to be about thirty-five. . . .

MULVEY
Uh . . . huh . . .

Phone RINGS.

> MULVEY
>> (into phone)
> Lieutenant Mulvey . . .
>> (listens with interest)
> Yes. . . . Yes. . . .
>> (face falls)
> Oh. . . . All right.
>> (hangs up; to Niles)
> Well, Mr. Niles, after telling me a lot of stories about a lot of things, you apparently told me an accurate story of where you were last night. Four witnesses put you at the Trinidad Club at the time Jean Dexter died.
>> (a gesture)
> I guess you're in the clear, Mr. Niles.

> NILES
>> (wearily)
> I told you I never lie about important things . . . Any more questions?

> MULVEY
> I guess not.

Niles rises, starts to go, stops.

> NILES
> You know—I'm not as much of a heel as I sound. I'm trying to catch on to a good job in industry. One of these days I will.

> MULVEY
>> (softly)
> I wish you the best.

> NILES
> Good-bye, then.

> MULVEY
> Good luck.

Niles leaves. Door closes.

> MULVEY
>> (continuing—softly to Perelli)

Keep two men on him in three shifts.
Perelli nods, leaves.

> MULVEY
> (to Miller)
> I don't want a thing said to the newspapers about Niles.
> He's not even in this case.

Miller nods.

> MULVEY
> (continuing)
> Spent fifty dollars last night, he said. On that much a week
> I supported a wife and raised two kids.

> HALLORAN
> Sure, but you were brought up on the wrong side of the
> tracks.

Mulvey smiles slightly.

EXT   HOMICIDE SQUAD BUILDING   DAY
Niles exits, putting on his coat. He trudges wearily down the street.

Two detectives come out of building, start slowly after Niles.

EXT   THE SAME STREET   DAY
Garza is standing near a hot dog and ice cream wagon that travels the
streets. He is sucking a popsicle and watching Niles. He turns and
goes the other way.

INT   MULVEY'S OFFICE   DAY
CAMERA PULLS BACK to REVEAL Mulvey, Miller, Halloran—in
consultation. Present as a special audience is Donahue. There is a
portable blackboard in office, on which are written the following
names:

> MARTHA SWENSON   PHILIP HENDERSON
> NED HARVEY
> RUTH YOUNG
> ROBERT NILES

Miller is talking, reading from his notebook.

> MILLER
> The only good fingerprints we got were of the maid and
> Jean Dexter . . . The Baltimore police say they can't locate

anyone so far who answers Henderson's description . . .
The pajamas in Dexter's apartment show nothing under the
X-ray. They're an English import and never been washed.
All stores that carry the line are being checked.
(looks up—to Donahue)
That's it, Captain.

DONAHUE
(to Mulvey)
Very little to go on. This man Niles . . . how's his alibi for
last night?

MULVEY
He seems in the clear. So does everybody else we've con-
nected with so far.

HALLORAN
So Henderson's our only suspect. . . .

MULVEY
How about this man?
Mulvey crosses to the blackboard, picks up chalk. Underneath Hen-
derson's name he writes:
JOSEPH P. McGILLICUDDY

HALLORAN
Who's he?

DONAHUE
(smiling)
McGillicuddy is Dan's name for any unknown party in a
case.

HALLORAN
You mean *two* men did the murder?

MULVEY
Maybe there were five. All I know is there was more than
one.

HALLORAN
How do you know?
Mulvey looks around the room, then sits on his desk. He pats it.

MULVEY

This is a bed . . . For a moment, I'm an attractive little lady.
(smiles to Halloran)
How would you chloroform me, Mr. Henderson?

Halloran studies the question, takes a handkerchief out of his pocket.

HALLORAN

I guess the best way'd be if I stood behind you.

He goes behind Mulvey and gestures how he would lock his forearm
over Mulvey's throat, and use the other hand to apply the chloroform.

MULVEY

Correct—that's the way one man *would* do it.

He jumps down, opens drawer, brings out a pile of 8 by 10 photos,
shuffles them, selects one. Meanwhile, he keeps talking.

MULVEY
(continuing)

We just got the photographs. They show finger marks on
both arms.

He tosses a photo on desk. All crowd around it.

INSERT PHOTO

It shows chin, neck, shoulders only. Visible are some blue marks.

MULVEY'S VOICE
(over close shot)

That means a man stood behind her and held her arms with
both hands, while Henderson or someone else chloroformed
her. A strong man, with thick, strong fingers.

INT BACK TO SCENE DAY

All look up from photo, gaze at Mulvey with excitement.

MULVEY
(continuing)

And that man was my old, old friend, Joseph P.
McGillicuddy.

A pause.

DONAHUE

You're right, Dan.

HALLORAN

Now we have to find two men.

DONAHUE

You have to find them. I'm busy on half a dozen other cases.
Goodnight, gentlemen.

ALL

Good night.

Donahue leaves.

MILLER

Need me any more?

Mulvey waves him good night. Miller goes. Mulvey looks at
blackboard.

MULVEY

A heavy case . . .
    (thinks)
Why is Niles such a liar?
    (pause)
What's in his heart? Is he just a blowhard or . . . ?
    (pause)
A heavy case. . . .

The door opens, Miller appears, wearing hat.

MILLER

    (excitedly)
Say . . . there's an old dame outside says she can crack the
Dexter case.

Mulvey gestures for her to be brought in. Miller steps out, ushers in
a sweet-faced old lady of sixty-five. She is dressed in an old-fashioned
manner and, in spite of the heat, wears a feather boa around her neck.
She has a folded newspaper under her arm. She speaks with a Southern accent.

OLD LADY

Are you the officer in charge of the bathtub murder?

MULVEY

Yes, M'am.

OLD LADY

    (approaching)

This one?

She spreads the newspaper on the desk.

INSERT NEWSPAPER HEADLINES

> Blonde Model Slain
> In Brutal Bathtub Killing

MULVEY'S VOICE

Yes, M'am.

INT BACK TO SCENE DAY

OLD LADY

I can help you solve it.

MULVEY

Yes?

OLD LADY

My gran'daddy is Sheriff of Tuckahue County, Mississippi. He's . . .

HALLORAN

(gasping)
Your gran'daddy?

Mulvey puts his hand out and touches Halloran warningly.

OLD LADY

(explaining)
Yes . . . I'm only in my twenties, you know.

MULVEY

(gently)
And very handsome you are, too.

OLD LADY

(candidly)
Yes, I know. So many men are crazy about me, I don't know what to do.
(starts to leave)
'Bye now.
(stops—hesitates)
Oh yes—about the murder. I almost forgot. We'll have to get a front tooth from a hound dog.

MULVEY

Yes, M'am.

OLD LADY

Bury it fifty feet from the grave. On the third day after the
first full moon, the murderer will confess.

MULVEY

Thank you, M'am.

OLD LADY
(starts off—then stops)
Prices are awfully high these days, aren't they?

MULVEY

Yes, M'am.

OLD LADY

I had to decide whether to spend a nickel on an apple for
my supper—or spend it on the subway to come up here.
Mulvey fishes in his pocket, comes up with a dime, gives it to her.

MULVEY

Please.

OLD LADY

You're sweet. I'll put you down in my diary tonight. 'Bye
now.

MULVEY

'Bye.
The old lady leaves. Miller gives them a look, also leaves. Mulvey and
Halloran look at each other.

HALLORAN

How much of that have you had in thirty-eight years?

MULVEY

I couldn't count it. Every time there's a headline case. We'll
be lucky if there isn't a lot more.

HALLORAN

'Bye now.

MULVEY
(grinning)
'Bye.

Halloran leaves. Mulvey turns to blackboard, looks at names. He erases all the names except those of Henderson, Niles, McGillicuddy. He stares at them.

EXT 14TH ST. DAY
Hurrying people are exiting from a department store.

NARRATOR
The day's work is over now . . .

EXT ANOTHER STREET DAY
Office workers are exiting from factory building at 99 Hudson Street.

. . . and several million people . . .

EXT QUEENSBORO BRIDGE DAY
A subway train is going over bridge.

. . . are on their way home . . .

INT SUBWAY CAR DAY FULL SHOT PEOPLE

. . . tired and hot . . .

INSERT A SITTING MAN
eyes closed, face sweaty.

Six A.M. tomorrow will come awfully soon.

INSERT A SITTING GIRL
young. She is staring, fasci-nated, at a tabloid and biting her fingernail.

Must've been a hard day behind that counter, honey . . .

INSERT TABLOID
There is a lurid drawing of the murder being committed *in* the bathtub. Very wild.

. . . but don't bite your nails. Harry won't like it. And be-sides, this isn't how the murder was really committed.

A CAPTION OVER IT
SAYS:"ARTIST'S CONCEPTION OF HOW MODEL DIED."

INT BACK TO SCENE DAY
Halloran, hanging onto a strap, is reading a paper. Behind him are a stout girl and a young man. The stout girl is short and is peering at Halloran's paper from under his arm.

STOUT GIRL
Read about that bathtub murder?

YOUNG MAN
I'll say. Some figger that dame had. I wouldna minded
being the wash rag in her bathtub. Haw! Haw!

EXT   AT A BILLBOARD   DAY
A newsboy has walked away from his stand to pencil a moustache
on the face of an actress in a movie advertisement . . . Passersby on
street.

NEWSBOY
(mechanically, as he draws . . . in double talk)
Evening paper . . . Sensational . . . Tibet Report . . . Bathtub murder . . . Hitler reported hiding in . . . Artist's Model
. . . Get your paper. . . .
Garza comes up, takes a paper, drops a nickel, walks off. A well-
dressed man takes a paper. As he is fishing for change he observes
newsboy with back turned. He walks off quickly without paying, a
pleased smirk on his face.

EXT   HALLORAN'S HOME   DAY
as he opens door of his two-family home and enters.

HALLORAN
(calling)
Anybody home?

He throws his hat and newspaper on the couch and starts taking off coat. The room is combination living-room, dining-room with standard Grand Rapids furniture. The small table is set for dinner. In answer to his call, a voice comes from the kitchen.

JANEY'S VOICE (OS)
Hello, honey.

She appears at kitchen door and comes toward him. She has on a playsuit with bare mid-riff and an apron. She is pretty in a quiet way, has a straightforward manner. Halloran pulls off tie and starts unbuttoning shirt.

JANEY
(continuing)
Bet it was hot in Manhattan today.

HALLORAN
I was too busy to be hot. On a new case.
(as he takes off shirt)
The subway was a furnace, though.

JANEY
You too warm to say hello?

HALLORAN
Yup.

He puts his arms around her, kisses her.

JANEY
Got you a nice, cool supper. Jellied tongue.

HALLORAN
(holding her)
Swell. I'm hungry. Stop holding on to me. Let's go, I'm starved.

She laughs. He kisses her, lets her go.

HALLORAN
(continuing)
Where's Billy?

                              JANEY
        I put him to bed. Listen, dear, I'm sorry to tell you but
        you've got a nasty job to do before supper.
Halloran takes off the hip belt on which his gun holster hangs and
puts it up on the closet shelf. Janey continues meanwhile.

                              JANEY
                           (continuing)
        Billy has to have a whipping.

                             HALLORAN
        Why?

                              JANEY
        He walked right out of the yard, crossed Stillman Avenue
        all by himself and went to the park.

                             HALLORAN
        Well . . . I'll give him a real talking to.

                              JANEY
        No you won't, you'll give him a real whipping, with a strap.

                             HALLORAN
        Just a minute, honey . . .

                              JANEY
                          (interrupting)
        I know—I know—you don't believe in whipping a child.
        Neither have I until now. But do you want Billy run over by
        a truck?
Halloran is silent.

                              JANEY
                           (continuing)
        I've reasoned with him, I've pleaded with him, I've threat-
        ened him. But the minute my back is turned, he's off.

                             HALLORAN
        Well . . . he's a spunky kid, Janey.

                              JANEY
        I don't want him to be a dead kid.

                             HALLORAN
                            (yielding)
        No . . .

JANEY

Go ahead then. Get it over with.

HALLORAN

Yeah, I guess I will . . . right after supper.

JANEY

Jimmy—
(points)

HALLORAN

I can't just go in there and take a strap to that boy. I've got to work up to it a little bit.

JANEY

You'd think I was asking you to kill him.

Phone RINGS.

HALLORAN

If *you* think it's so easy, you whip him.
(goes to phone)

JANEY

Me? That's not a *woman's* job.

HALLORAN

(at phone)
Why does it have to be a man's job?

JANEY

It's always the man's job.

HALLORAN

(raising phone)
Who says so? . . . Hello.
(listens)
Oh . . . sure, Dan . . . yeah, right away.

He hangs up, crosses to closet for gun.

HALLORAN

Got a call. I have to meet Mulvey right away.

JANEY

Without any supper?

HALLORAN

Save it for me . . . I'll grab a hamburger meanwhile.

JANEY

I wish you were an ice cream salesman or something. I don't like this night work and I don't like it every time you strap on that gun.

Halloran is now putting on his shirt and tie. Janey takes off her apron.

HALLORAN

If I were an ice cream salesman, I'd get fat. Then you wouldn't like me.

JANEY

I don't like you now.

HALLORAN
(singing it)
Oh, yes you do.

JANEY

Remember—you've got a job before you leave this house.

HALLORAN

What?

JANEY

Billy.

HALLORAN

I can't stop for that now.

JANEY
(jumping up)
Halloran—you're a coward.

HALLORAN
(kissing her)
'Bye now.

He grabs coat and starts off.

JANEY

Jimmy.

He stops. She goes up and catches his arm, kisses him.

JANEY
(continuing)
I'll wait up for you.

HALLORAN

Good deal.

He runs his finger across her bare midriff. She wiggles a little.

JANEY

Where you going?

HALLORAN

To see a pretty girl.

He runs his finger across her midriff again. She wiggles.

JANEY

Some place exciting, huh?

HALLORAN

Yes, dear. To the morgue.

He pokes her with his finger, starts out.

DISSOLVE TO:

EXT BUILDING MARKED: CITY MORTUARY NIGHT
as Detective Constentino approaches with a plainly dressed, middle-aged couple, the Batorys. The man and woman stare at the sign for a moment and then follow Constentino inside.

INT ANTEROOM OF MORTUARY NIGHT MULVEY, HALLORAN AND UNIFORMED NURSE
are seated, but rise when Constentino enters with the man and woman. Constentino is forty-five, husky, dark, competent appearing. Mr. Batory is fifty, thin, looking both strong and work-worn, with a neat little grey moustache and a bald head. Mrs. Batory is the same age, stocky, with a face and figure that show signs of an earlier peasant beauty. Mr. Batory looks stunned, grief-stricken, shocked beyond understanding. Mrs. Batory seems at the point of hysteria, her eyes red, her hands plucking at her dress, her hair, her face.

CONSTENTINO

This is Lieutenant Mulvey.
(to Mulvey)
Mr. and Mrs. Batory, the girl's parents.

Before Mulvey can say anything, Mrs. Batory bursts out in an angry, injured, bitter tone.

MRS. BATORY

I told her! I knew she'd turn out no good. All these young

girls . . . so crazy to be with the bright lights. There's no
bright lights for her now, is there?
> (she stops, plucks at her dress)

                    MULVEY
> (gently)
She's at rest now, Mrs. Batory.

                    MRS. BATORY
> (bitterly)
No—her kind of dead don't rest! And how 'bout us? The
scandal—God in Heaven! My husband's a gardener. He
works for a banker, a highly respectable gentleman. He'll
get fired now. Oh, I hate her, I hate her.

                    MR. BATORY
> (miserably)
Paula . . .

                    MRS. BATORY
Never mind . . . I hate her. I say it out straight. So fancy she
was. Even had to change her name. Hah!

                    MULVEY
> (uncomfortably)
We'd better go in now. If you'll please follow the nurse.

FOLLOW SHOT
as nurse leads the way down a short hallway and into a room. The
group follows. CAMERA is CLOSE on MRS. BATORY, who keeps muttering as she walks.

                    MRS. BATORY
I do hate her, I do. I warned her. A million times I warned
her.

INT MORTUARY NIGHT
as group enters room. In the center is a table on which lies a covered
body, the face out of CAMERA range. The Batorys stop dead. Mrs.
Batory continues to mutter.

                    MRS. BATORY
I hate her. I hate her for what she done to us.
Mulvey gestures to nurse. She walks toward body to raise sheet from
face.

MULVEY
(to Batorys)
Please tell me if she's your daughter.

CLOSE SHOT BATORYS
Mrs. Batory falls silent. An instant later we see by the reaction on both their faces that the face of the dead girl has been exposed. Mr. Batory seems to shrink back, become smaller. Mrs. Batory's lips quiver.

MR. BATORY
(dully)
That's her . . .
Mrs. Batory stands with trembling lips. Her hand plucks at her dress, her face. A sudden, hysterical scream bursts from her lips.

MRS. BATORY
My baby! Oh, my baby!
She runs forward.

INT AT THE TABLE NIGHT
Mrs. Batory throws herself on foot of table, sobbing brokenly. The nurse is replacing the sheet.

EXT   DEAD END STREET OVERLOOKING RIVER   NIGHT
as Mr. and Mrs. Batory come up to bench. She sits down, he sits
beside her. Behind them are Mulvey and Halloran. Mulvey pauses
near them, begins stuffing a pipe. Halloran leans against a lamppost,
smokes a cigarette. A police sedan, with Constentino and a driver,
pauses a bit down the street.

> MRS. BATORY
> (low-voiced)
> I feel better now. The walk was good for me.

> MULVEY
> Are you sure you want to go home tonight? We can get you
> a hotel room.

Batory looks at his wife, then shakes his head.

> MR. BATORY
> We'll go home. We don't like this place . . .
> (bitterly)
> . . . this fine city.

> MRS. BATORY
> (diffidently—to Mulvey)
> You don't know . . . who done it, huh?

> MULVEY
> Not yet.

He fishes in his pocket, brings out the black star sapphire ring that
was on Jean Dexter's hand. He steps closer to them, shows it.

> MULVEY
> (continuing)
> Did you ever see this?

The Batorys look at it, shake their heads.

> MULVEY
> (continuing)
> Your daughter told someone it came from her brother, in
> India.

> MR. BATORY
> (confused)
> We only had her—no other kids—no boy.

Mulvey looks at Halloran, puts ring in pocket.

MULVEY

I see . . . And did your daughter ever mention a man named
Henderson?

MRS. BATORY

(bitterly)

We don't know any Henderson. We haven't seen Mary even
for six months. She was too busy to come see us. Who
knows what she ran around with?

MR. BATORY

(to his wife)

She's dead, momma, don't . . .

(to Mulvey, passionately)

A good girl, I swear it! It's my fault maybe I didn't do better
for her. When she was fifteen she was working already, the
five and ten cent store. Oh it was hard, depression time,
hard.

MRS. BATORY

(to her husband)

So what? She's the only one didn't have it easy? Other people had it worse! Was that a reason to leave home—to change
your name?

(to Mulvey)

Wanting too much, that's why she went wrong. Bright lights
and thee-aters and furs and night clubs. That's why she's
dead now. Dear God, why wasn't she born ugly?

(begins to weep quietly)

What a heartache! You nurse a child, raise it, pet it, love it
. . . and it ends like this.

MULVEY

I've had my own children, Mrs. Batory. They turned out all
right, thank goodness, but who's to know why or how? I've
seen a lot of human misery in my work. *I* don't know where
people start to go wrong.

MRS. BATORY

(defensively)

We did our best. It wasn't *our* fault.

MULVEY

Of course it wasn't. And maybe not even hers. When you
think it over, I guess it was everybody's fault. People get so
pounded and pounded in this life.
(shakes his head—softly)
It's a jungle, a city like this. Eight million people struggling
for life, for food, for air, for a bit of happiness. Seems like
there ain't enough of everything to go around . . . and so
sometimes it breaks out in . . . violence.

A boat whistle blows mournfully from the river. Mulvey looks out
over the water.

MULVEY
(continuing in a murmur)
. . . an' we call it homicide . . .

FADE OUT

FADE IN
EXT TALL BUILDINGS DAY
SUNRISE STREAMING OVER
THE TOWERS OF LOWER
MANHATTAN

NARRATOR
Six A.M.—Summer day—work
day.

EXT THE SKY DAY
A flight of birds across CAMERA.

This time yesterday, Jean Dexter
was just another name in the
phone book . . .

INT A CAFETERIA DAY A
MAN
is reading a tabloid. Shoves toast
in his mouth.

. . . but now she's the marma-
lade on ten thousand pieces of
toast . . .

INT APARTMENT DOOR DAY
In front of door is a folded newspaper, and a bottle of coffee
cream standing on a piece of note
paper. The door opens. We hear
a voice, half humming, half singing. Mulvey appears, in trousers, slippers, no shirt,
suspenders hanging. He picks up
newspaper, bottle, note.

. . . all around the town . . .

MULVEY
East Side, West Side, all around
the town . . .

INT MULVEY'S APARTMENT DAY
Still humming, he carries things back to table. He opens note.

INSERT: NOTE:
> Dear Mr. Mulvey:
> Sorry the cream was sour yesterday. About this new case you're on—I figure it's the janitor—a sex crime. Do you want any buttermilk?
>
> Your Milkman.

INT MULVEY DAY
He hums, grins, pours cream in coffee.

INT DRUGSTORE DAY
The druggist is serving grapefruit and coffee to a man at the counter.

DRUGGIST

So I says to that detective: 'Confidentially,' I says, 'that Dexter girl used to come in here night after night and pour her heart out to me—ask my advice.' That'll be twenty-five cents, please. And I told her 'marry and settle down, have a couple kids,' I said! But it's too late now.
(leans forward)
Keep it confidential, bud, willya?

INT STONEMAN DINING ROOM DAY
Dr. Stoneman and his wife, eating breakfast. He is dressed, she is in negligee, a woman of fifty. Both are reading newspapers.

MRS. STONEMAN

(suddenly)
Lawrence!!

STONEMAN

(reading)
Uh-huh?

MRS. STONEMAN

This Dexter murder case! It says she was your patient.

STONEMAN

Not really. I only saw her once.

MRS. STONEMAN

She was beautiful, wasn't she?

STONEMAN

Quite.

MRS. STONEMAN

What was she like?

STONEMAN

Just one of those sad creatures who want more than life can give them.
      (raising coffee urn)
Coffee?

INT   EDITORIAL OFFICE OF A NEWSPAPER   DAY
Publisher, managing editor.

PUBLISHER

This Dexter case. Give it an editorial today. 'What's the matter with the police? What's the matter with the Mayor?' Slam into 'em. Pin their ears back.

MANAGING EDITOR

How about saying the whole city's in the grip of a crime wave?

PUBLISHER

Listen—as long as this administration's in office, we're suffering from a perpetual crime wave.

MANAGING EDITOR

Check.

INT   ANOTHER NEWSPAPER OFFICE   DAY
Another managing editor, another publisher.

MANAGING EDITOR

How do you want me to handle the Dexter case editorially?

PUBLISHER

You know our policy. Watch how the *Tabloid* handles it. You do the opposite.

MANAGING EDITOR

Check.

EXT   JEAN DEXTER'S APARTMENT HOUSE   DAY
A small crowd of people is gawking in front. A policeman stands at

door. A vendor with a peanut, ice-cream and hotdog stand is at the curb, doing business.

Random voices are heard:

> FIRST MAN'S VOICE
> Hey, Mac—what's doin', why all the people here?

> SECOND MAN'S VOICE
> (genially)
> What's doin? Whatsamatter, you live in Canarsie or somethin'? This is the dump where that model was killed.

> FIRST MAN'S VOICE
> You don't mean it! The bathtub girl, eh? So why didn't she take showers?

Both men laugh.

EXT   CITY HALL   DAY

INT   OFFICE CORRIDOR   DAY
One office door reads:
> OFFICE OF THE MAYOR

INT   MAYOR'S OFFICE   DAY

> THE MAYOR
> (to reporters)
> That's all for this morning, gentlemen. Any questions?

> A REPORTER
> Since Commissioner Wallander's here, do you have any statement on the Jean Dexter case?

> THE MAYOR
> I don't. Do you, Commissioner?

> COMMISSIONER WALLANDER
> (genially)
> A case is a case. If it happens to lend itself to sensationalism, that's your good luck. But to the Homicide Squad, it's just another job.

> THE MAYOR
> I'll tell you this: As Mayor of New York I expect criticism—not only of me but of the Police Department. But as an ex-cop, I know a tough case when I see one. Not many murders

go unsolved—but it takes more than twenty-four hours to handle a case like this.

COMMISSIONER WALLANDER
(to Mayor)
For that—thanks.

THE MAYOR
Don't mention it.
(smiles)

EXT MADISON AVE DAY
Niles, wearing the phony rup-tured duck in the lapel of a Pan-ama suit, comes down the street, enters a jewelry store.

NARRATOR
The sun isn't too hot as yet. And it's pleasant to walk along Madi-son Ave . . .

EXT TWO MEN ON MADISON AVE. DAY CAMERA IS SHOOTING ACROSS AND DOWN THE STREET
The two men are looking toward CAMERA. They step into a doorway.

. . . there are shady doorways to rest in . . . for patient men who are not in a hurry.

EXT EAST SIDE ST. DAY
A hurdy gurdy player.

SOUND: He is grinding out "After the Ball is Over."

It's pleasant on an early summer morning to listen to an old song . . .

A coin bounces down on side-walk, rolls. A passerby picks it up, gives it to hurdy gurdy man—walks off. The passerby is Garza.

. . . it whiles away the time.

EXT AN EAST SIDE PIER DAY
where several adolescent boys are stripping off their clothes for a swim. They wear tights un-derneath. The first boy, un-dressed, steps up to the edge of the pier, ready to dive. Suddenly he yells out and points.

NARRATOR
. . . So pleasant to dive into the East River even though some-times the water is littered with a city's trash: a half-eaten apple . . . a chip of wood . . . a lady's hat . . .

BOY

The other boys run up, look
down into water.

Look! Hey, look!

NARRATOR   (softly)

EXT   A MAN'S BODY IN WATER
DAY
floating face downward.

. . . a chip of wood . . . a lady's
hat . . . and other things. . . .

INT   OUTER OFFICE OF PRECINCT HEADQUARTERS   DAY
Perelli. He goes toward door marked 'Lieutenant Mulvey', enters.

INT   MULVEY'S OFFICE   DAY
Mulvey, at desk, Constentino, Halloran. Mulvey is talking.

MULVEY

This is Dexter's address book. Contact every name listed
in it. Keep asking if they heard her talk about Henderson.
Constentino nods, takes the address book, leaves. Mulvey nods to
Perelli.

MULVEY

(to Halloran)
Start in on this ring of Dexter's.
(takes out black star sapphire)
Canvass every expensive jewelry shop in the city . . . maybe
Henderson bought it for her.

HALLORAN

(grinning)
Oh, my poor feet.

MULVEY

(smiling)
Be glad you're not a horseback cop.
Halloran leaves.

MULVEY

(to Perelli)
What's with you?

PERELLI

(takes a man's diamond-studded cigarette case out
of his pocket)
Niles sold this about an hour ago to a jeweler on Madison
Avenue. Got six hundred dollars for it.

MULVEY
(excited)
Well! Where's the list of stuff that was stolen from Dexter?
He opens a desk drawer, pulls out a typewritten sheet of paper. He examines cigarette case, looks down list.

MULVEY
(disappointed)
It isn't on here. It's a man's item anyway.
Perelli grimaces in disappointment.

MULVEY
(slowly)
That's an interesting man, that Niles. He operates very strange.

PERELLI
Say—how about I check this cigarette case with the Department list of all jewelry stolen in the last year or so?

MULVEY
All right . . . I don't think you'll get anything, though. He'd be crazy to pawn a *stolen* item in the middle of a hot case like this.

PERELLI
Maybe he is crazy.
(rises)

MULVEY
Not that one.
Perelli leaves.

Mulvey sits thinking, stuffs a pipe.

NARRATOR
(softly) Button, button, who's got the button?

EXT A BEAUTY SHOP ON LEX-INGTON AVENUE DAY
Constentino stops outside, checks number.

Relax, Constentino, your wife does this, too.

He steps inside and blinks a little at the spectacle of eight women in a row sitting under

. . . How about a permanent, bud? How about a mud-pack for your complexion? Ever have your

dryers. All of the women, naturally, turn as one to stare at him. An operator walks up to him. They talk for a moment. The operator shakes her head several times. Constentino leaves.

eyebrows plucked? What? Don't you even get your nails manicured? Hey, Constentino, wait! You could get to like it here.

INT FASHIONABLE JEWELRY SHOP DAY
Jeweler and Halloran—Jeweler is looking at the black star sapphire ring.

JEWELER
No, I never saw this ring. It's an odd one. Hard to forget.

HALLORAN
Thanks. You've been a help.

EXT OUTSIDE JEWELRY SHOP DAY
Halloran emerges, looks at list of stores on paper. He starts off.

NARRATOR
How are the feet, Halloran? Would you care for some arch supporters? Would you be interested in knowing that there was a confession in this case only ten minutes ago?

EXT FIFTY-SEVENTH STREET DAY
A police car is racing through traffic, siren wide open.

NARRATOR
What's your hurry, Mulvey? You're supposed to be a patient man. Why get so excited?

INT MEN'S HABERDASHERY SHOP ON LEXINGTON AVENUE DAY
A detective is standing with the proprietor, who is examining Henderson's pajamas.

Calling all members of the Homicide Squad, Officer. There was a confession in the Dexter case at 11:50 A.M.

EXT TOOTS SHOR'S RESTAURANT DAY
Constentino is consulting address book. He starts in.

Hey, Constentino—why don't you throw that address book away? This case is all washed up—it's finished—got a confession—

INT LIVING ROOM OF DEXTER'S APARTMENT DAY
Sitting down, head in his hands, is BISBEE, a tall, gaunt young man
who speaks in a reedy voice. A policeman is opening the door. Mulvey and Miller burst in.

POLICEMAN
(excitedly)
Here he is, Lieutenant. I caught him trying to get in the
kitchen by the back door. He's a grocery boy in the
neighborhood.

Bisbee jumps up.

BISBEE
Yes, I did it—I killed her. I want to be punished. I'm guilty.
My hands are stained with her blood.

MULVEY
Why did you kill her?

BISBEE
She deserved it. For months I've been watching her. I'd
come up with packages and there she'd be—in her negligee—beautiful—but no soul—immoral. So I did it. I rid the
world of her.

MULVEY
(quickly)
The knife you stabbed her with. What did you do with it?

BISBEE
You'll never find it—never. I buried it—I buried it.

MULVEY
(to Cop)
Call Bellevue Hospital . . . Psychiatric Department.
(starts out)

DISSOLVE:

INT MULVEY'S OFFICE NIGHT
MULVEY, DONAHUE, MILLER
Miller is cleaning his fingernails
with a penknife. Donahue is
looking over various reports that

NARRATOR
It's seven-thirty in the evening
now. It's been a great day on the
Dexter case: Developments—
none; new clues—none; prog-

Mulvey is handing him from a folder. ress—none. Ever try to catch a murderer? It has its depressing moments.

Donahue now returns the last report to Mulvey. Mulvey closes the folder. Donahue rubs his forefinger thoughtfully up and down the length of his nose.

> DONAHUE
>
> I can't see you've missed anything.

> MULVEY
>
> (wryly)
> Boss, I can always trust you to comfort a man.

Pause.

> DONAHUE
>
> Any word today from Baltimore?

> MULVEY
>
> No . . . and Henderson's pajamas were bought last week in a store on 34th Street—but not by Henderson—by Jean Dexter.

Pause. Donahue shakes his head.

> DONAHUE
>
> A heavy case . . .

> MULVEY
>
> It's that.

The door opens. Perelli appears, looking very pleased. He takes the cigarette case sold by Niles out of his pocket.

> PERELLI
>
> This cigarette case Niles sold this morning—it's hot. It was stolen from Dr. Lawrence Stoneman.

> DONAHUE
>
> Dexter's physician?

> PERELLI
>
> Yeah. He reported a robbery in his apartment in March. Twenty-eight hundred dollars worth of stuff. None of it has ever shown up . . . Here's the Department list of stolen jewelry for the past year.

He hands some typewritten sheets to Mulvey. Mulvey's eyes are gleaming. The atmosphere of the office has completely altered, from defeat to excitement.

PERELLI
(continuing)
That's not all—Niles bought a plane ticket for Mexico City—one way.

MULVEY
Leaving when?

PERELLI
Tomorrow noon . . . Want me to pick him up?

MULVEY
No. What else did he do today?

PERELLI
. . . Had lunch with Ruth Young. They held hands for an hour. She went back to her shop—he went to the Park Central and had a swim. He's at Toots Shor's now.

DONAHUE
(amused)
Buying a plane ticket—pawning a stolen cigarette case—that's not smart. What is this man—an amachoor or something?

MULVEY
(slaps the palm of his hand on the table)
That's what's in his heart! Now I know! He's had no experience at being a crook. He's a scared college boy way out in deep water. He's starting to thrash around now, he's in a panic.

DONAHUE
A panic over what?

MULVEY
I don't know, yet, Sam.

DONAHUE
(excitedly)
And how does this Stoneman figure? Why should Niles pawn a cigarette case belonging to him?

Door opens suddenly. Halloran strides in, excited.

> HALLORAN

Dan—I got something, maybe.

> MULVEY

About what?

> HALLORAN

The black star sapphire Dexter was wearing when she was killed—it didn't belong to her. She didn't buy it, Henderson didn't buy it for her. It belongs to a Mrs. Hylton, 482 Park Ave. I found a jeweler who repaired it for her.

Excitedly Mulvey picks up the Department list of stolen jewelry. Perelli looks over his shoulder. Mulvey turns a page, then another.

> DONAHUE

> (muttering)

We started in a murder case and we're up to our necks in stolen jewery.

> PERELLI

> (suddenly . . . pointing)

Mrs. Edgar Hylton—there it is.

> MULVEY

> (excitedly)

Black star sapphire—part of a sixty-two-hundred-dollar robbery of her apartment.

> (to Halloran)

Did you see this Mrs. Hylton?

> HALLORAN

I thought *you* might want to see her.

> MULVEY

Now that was considerate of you, Jimmy. We'll telephone the lady and we'll both go to see her.

He turns to Donahue with gleaming eyes.

> MULVEY

Have a beer on me, Sam. An' throw a pinch of salt over your shoulder. This case is starting to move.

EXT IN FRONT OF 482 PARK AVENUE NIGHT	NARRATOR Ever watch a hound dog tracking

A police sedan stops at the curb. Mulvey and Halloran get out, walk toward entrance.

down a rabbit? It sniffs—and sniffs—and suddenly it begins to run . . .

INT   APARTMENT HOUSE CORRIDOR   NIGHT
Mulvey and Halloran are entering an apartment. A maid has opened the door.

INT   FOYER OF HYLTON APARTMENT   NIGHT
A rhumba record is being played in an adjacent room.

MAID

     Mrs. Hylton's waiting for you.

She leads the way to a sitting room, separated from the foyer by heavy brocade curtains.

INT   SITTING ROOM   NIGHT
as they enter. Rhumba music is coming over the radio. MRS. HYLTON is sitting by the radio, her head cocked to one side, listening to the music with obvious delight. She gestures for them to come in but continues to listen to the music, which is approaching the end of a tune. One foot is tapping out the rhythm. Mulvey and Halloran exchange amused glances, wait. The music ends, Mrs. Hylton switches off the radio, then jumps up and comes toward them, beaming.

She is a woman in her late forties, no more than five feet tall, very slim, bright-eyed. Her speech, her gestures, her walk, are all very quick, vigorous; she is as close to being a hummingbird as any woman can be. She is dressed in an attractive, expensive house-coat and is wearing diamond rings on both hands, a diamond bracelet, a diamond clip in her grey hair.

> MAID
>
> Lieutenant Mulvey, M'am.
> (she leaves)

> MRS. HYLTON
>
> (gayly)
> As you see, I'm crazy about rhumba music. Imagine, at my age!
> (to Halloran)
> My, what a nice-looking young man!
> (to Mulvey)
> You're the Lieutenant who telephoned me, aren't you? Did you get my jewels back?

Mulvey produces the black star sapphire.

> MULVEY
>
> Is this one of 'em?

> MRS. HYLTON
>
> (with a shriek of delight)
> Yes it is! Oh, wonderful, you wonderful men. Where's the rest?

> MULVEY
>
> This is all we have.

> MRS. HYLTON
>
> I'm so disappointed! But this is wonderful. I gave it to my daughter when she graduated from college. She was heart-broken when—
> (stops talking . . . holds ring up to light)
> Isn't it precious?
> (laughs . . . holds out hands)
> I love to glitter. It's a fixation.
> (to Halloran)
> My, you're nice looking.
> (gesturing)

Sit down, gentlemen, get comfortable.
Mulvey and Halloran sit. Both of them look a bit bewildered.

MULVEY

Mrs. Hylton—is your daughter here? I'd like to talk to her.

MRS. HYLTON

(looking at wrist watch)
She's due any minute for dinner—it's her night with
Momma.
(laughs)
One of those career girls—has her own apartment—works.
That's what you get when you send them to Vassar.
(laughs)

MULVEY

If she doesn't live with you, how is it her ring was stolen
from here?

MRS. HYLTON

That was last December. She *was* living with me then.

MULVEY

I see . . . Now . . . ah . . . I wonder if by any chance . . .

A GIRL'S VOICE

Mother? I'm here.
Ruth Young appears in the doorway. Halloran bounds to his feet.

HALLORAN

Niles—he's the connection!

MULVEY

Easy, lad.
(crossing to Ruth)
You told me your name was Ruth Young—not Hylton.

MRS. HYLTON

Ruth's my daughter by a first marriage. She kept her father's
name.
(to Ruth)
How do you know these men?

RUTH

They're investigating Jean Dexter's murder. Jean modeled
with me at the shop, Mother.

                        MRS. HYLTON
Imagine!
        (suddenly)
Look, darling.
        (displays sapphire)

                        RUTH
My ring!

                        MRS. HYLTON
They brought it. Aren't they wonderful?

                        RUTH
How did you get it?

                        MULVEY
Your friend was wearing it when she was murdered.

                        RUTH
        (bewildered)
Jean?

                        MRS. HYLTON
How did she get it?

                        MULVEY
I was hoping your daughter would tell us that.

                        RUTH
I have no idea. It was stolen with the other things.
        (suddenly, to Halloran)
What did you mean before when you said, 'Niles—he's the
connection?'
Halloran shifts awkwardly, says nothing.

                        RUTH
        (continuing)
What did you mean? Please . . .

                        MULVEY
He was just wondering, Miss . . . how your ring came to be
on *her* finger.

                        RUTH
You don't think Robert . . . ?

(laughs)
But that's silly. He hardly knew Jean.

MULVEY

That ring on your hand now . . . is it your engagement ring?

RUTH

Yes.

MULVEY

Might I see it?
Ruth takes it off, gives it to him.

MULVEY

(continuing)
A pearl in an old-fashioned setting. Unusual.
Mulvey gives ring and a list from his pocket to Halloran.

MULVEY

(continuing)
Jimmy—
Halloran nods, moves off a little, sits.

RUTH

(composed)
What are you doing?

MULVEY

(gently)
I'm sorry, Miss. We're checking your ring to see if it was stolen.

RUTH

(trying to be nice about it)
You don't mind if I feel rather insulted, do you?

MULVEY

(gently)
I'd expect you to.

MRS. HYLTON

I'm sure you have to question everyone who knew Miss Dexter—but this is fantastic.

RUTH

Do you honestly think either Robert or I had anything to do with her murder?

MULVEY

Just earning my salary, Miss.

Halloran suddenly steps up to Ruth.

HALLORAN

When did Niles give you this ring?

RUTH

About six weeks ago.

HALLORAN

On January 8th, Mrs. Charles Franklyn, 382 Fern Ave., New Rochelle, reported the loss of this ring in a robbery.

Ruth is stricken. She stares at him in horror. Mrs. Hylton looks stunned.

A pause.

RUTH

(rising . . . anguished)

Mother, if you don't mind, I won't have supper with you tonight.

MRS. HYLTON

Of course, dear.

(vaguely, to Mulvey)

Robert, a thief? But he's so educated. He studied philosophy in college . . .

Mulvey, however, is paying no attention to Mrs. Hylton. He calls sharply to Ruth Young, who has started out of the room.

MULVEY

Miss Young.

She pauses.

MULVEY

(continuing)

Where are you going?

RUTH

(in a whisper)

Whatever you're thinking, I know the sort of man Robert is.
There's some explanation of this, and he'll give it to me.

> MULVEY
>
> Okay—but we'll have to go with you.

> RUTH
>
> Oh!
> (pause)
> That's quite all right . . . Good-bye, Mother. I'll call you.

Her mother is too stricken to reply.

> MULVEY
>
> (on way out)
> Good night, M'am.

Mrs. Hylton stands, looking very distracted. The others leave. Her
hand goes to her face, plucks at her lip.

> MRS. HYLTON
>
> (to herself)
> Upsetting . . . everything's always so upsetting.

Maid appears at entrance.

> MAID
>
> Isn't Miss Ruth staying to supper?

> MRS. HYLTON
>
> No . . . no, she isn't . . . I'll eat alone . . .
> (starts out, pauses)
> Put on some music, Margaret . . . a rhumba.

EXT A STREET IN EAST EIGHTIES NIGHT
A taxi comes slowly down the street, stops. Mulvey steps out, looks
around. A figure comes out of the shadow of a building, joins him. It
is Perelli.

EXT MULVEY, PERELLI NIGHT
In BG in taxi, are Ruth Young and Halloran. Ruth is twisting a handkerchief in her hands.

> MULVEY
>
> (low-voiced)
> Is Niles in?

> PERELLI
>
> Went in about half an hour ago.

                    MULVEY
        Alone?

                    PERELLI
        Yeah.
Reaches in pocket, hands him a key.

                    PERELLI
                 (continuing)
        Apartment 7 E. Building on the corner.

                    MULVEY
        You can go home now.

                    PERELLI
        Thanks . . . I'm dead. S'long.

                    MULVEY
        Good night.
Perelli leaves. Mulvey beckons to Halloran. He and Ruth get out of
the car as Mulvey pays hackie. They start across the street, on the
diagonal, toward the corner apartment house.

INT APARTMENT HOUSE CORRIDOR NIGHT
Mulvey, Halloran, Ruth stop at a door. A spill of light underneath.
Halloran rings the bell. They wait. He rings the bell again. They
wait.

> MULVEY
>> (calling)
> Niles!

There is no reply. Mulvey takes the key out of his pocket. Halloran
takes out his gun.

> MULVEY
>> (sharply, to Ruth)
> Stand back.

He pushes her to one side. He opens door, flings it back and lets
Halloran rush in.

INT NILES APARTMENT NIGHT
as Halloran, Mulvey, with Ruth following, burst in. Niles is on the
floor, unconscious. A chair is overturned, the contents of a suitcase
are strewn all over a divan.

> MULVEY
>> The window!

Halloran races across the room to an open window, climbs out.

EXT FIRE ESCAPE NIGHT
as Halloran jumps out, looks down. Four stories below he sees a shad-
owy, bulky figure, racing down. The sound of pounding feet on the
iron grid work comes up. Halloran snaps up his gun, leans out,
shoots. There is an instant metallic ping as the bullet hits the fire escape somewhere down below, then ricochets with a shattering of glass
through a window in the house. Halloran starts to run down as a yell
comes from below. Above the pounding of Halloran's feet we hear an
angry man's voice.

> MAN'S VOICE
> What's going on here?

EXT HALLORAN'S FACE NIGHT
tense, breaking out with sweat, as he runs. We hear him panting for
breath.

A light switches on in a window as he runs past it. A window bangs
up.

> A WOMAN'S VOICE
> (screaming)
> Police—somebody call the police.
> (she repeats it several times)

EXT FIRE ESCAPE NIGHT
We see the two running figures from the sidewalk below. Halloran is now at the fifth floor; the man escaping is just at the edge of the ladder which forms the last section of fire escape. He swings down onto it; it slides down to the ground.

EXT GARZA NIGHT
face bathed in sweat, eyes gleaming, chest heaving. He fires twice at Halloran; the bullets slam into the grid work, ricochet. Garza starts to run out of the alley.

EXT GARZA NIGHT
from Halloran's POV. Halloran stops running, leans out, shoots. Garza keeps running, disappears into alley. Halloran runs again.

EXT HALLORAN NIGHT
Seen from below. Lights are going on all over the house. There is a babble of talk and shouts. Halloran comes to the last section. He swings with it to the pavement. He runs down the alley out into the deserted street. As he looks down one way a voice yells to him. It is from a man in pajamas in the window of a house opposite.

> MAN
> (yelling)
> What's going on there? What's the matter?

> HALLORAN
> (yelling)
> Police! Did you see a man run out of here?

> MAN
> That way! Around the corner!

Halloran runs around the corner. At the opposite corner is a subway entrance. He pounds down the street, runs down the subway steps.

INT SUBWAY PLATFORM (SHOOTING UP) NIGHT
as Halloran leaps down the last few stairs, gun in hand. CAMERA PANS WITH HIM as he vaults over the turnstiles. A train is pulling out of the station. The platform is deserted except for two elderly women

coming out of the exit. They cling together, stare at Halloran in horror as he hurries through turnstile over to an elderly station attendant who has not moved out of his booth.

> HALLORAN
> (excitedly)
> Police emergency! Is there any way of stopping that train at the next station—keeping the doors locked?

> ATTENDANT
> The train that just pulled out?
> (Halloran nods)
> Well, yes, I—I guess there is.
> (eager to help, but very ineffectual)
> Let's see now. I'd have to call the main office first . . .
> (reaches for phone)
> . . . or maybe I better call the 86th Street station. Which do you think?

> HALLORAN
> (wearily)
> Never mind. Thanks just the same.
> (puts away his gun; starts out)

INT NILES APARTMENT NIGHT
Niles is still on the floor, but there is a pillow under his head and his collar and tie have been opened. Ruth, on her knees, is bathing his face with a wet towel. A basin of water stands nearby. Mulvey is just crossing to the window as we hear shouts from the outside.

> A WOMAN'S VOICE
> Isn't anybody going to call the police?

> A MAN'S VOICE
> What for? Somebody found somebody else in the wrong apartment, that's all.
> (laughs)

> MULVEY
> (shouting out window)
> Listen to me, everybody—this is Lieutenant Mulvey of the Police Department talking. The trouble's all over. Get quiet now and go back to sleep.

He shuts window, returns to Ruth and Niles.

RUTH
(muttering)
Darling, darling . . . Robert, Robert.
(to Mulvey)
Maybe some whiskey would help.

MULVEY
(calmly)
Whiskey's not the thing to mix with chloroform. Suppose
you go into the kitchen and see if there's a spot of coffee on
the stove. It'll do fine, even if it's cold.

Ruth jumps up, runs out. Mulvey bends down, raises Niles's head
with one hand. He proceeds to slap him smartly on both sides of the
face.

MULVEY
(muttering)
Come on now, my sleepin' beauty . . . wake up.
(slapping him)
That's the sweet lad.
(slaps him)

Niles groans, his eyelids flutter, his head turns. Mulvey slaps him
again, then reaches for the basin of water. He pours the water over
Niles's face. Niles's eyes open in a bewildered stare. Ruth comes into
room carrying a cup.

RUTH
I found some cold tea.

MULVEY
That'll do fine. He's waking up now.

She runs to Niles, kneels.

RUTH
Robert, darling.

NILES
(still dazed)
Hello, Ruth.

She kisses him, holds, him, cradles him, kisses him again.

MULVEY
(muttering)
A touching scene.

(to Ruth)
The cold tea'll do him more good.
The door opens, Halloran comes in. Mulvey joins him. They whisper.
Halloran's face is wet with sweat.

HALLORAN
He got away. On the subway, I think.

MULVEY
Get a look at him?

HALLORAN
No. He was a big man—that's all I got. What do I smell in
here?

MULVEY
Chloroform. I think this is our friend McGillicuddy again.

HALLORAN
Oh!
They both move into room. Niles is sitting up now, drinking the tea
with Ruth's help.

MULVEY
You awake?
Niles nods. He starts to get up, groans.

NILES
I've got a head like a beehive.
He feels the back of his head over one ear, winces. Halloran takes him
under both arms from behind, lifts him. On wobbly knees Niles
makes a chair, sinks down into it.

NILES
(continuing)
Is that towel wet?

RUTH
(giving it to him)
Want any more tea, darling?

NILES
No.
He looks at Mulvey, rubs his face with the towel.

MULVEY

While you're thinking up a nice story about what didn't happen—suppose you tell us what did?

NILES

(slowly)

I don't know.

(rubs his face with towel)

MULVEY

(sarcastically)

Complete blackout, eh?

NILES

I was packing a bag and . . . I thought I heard a noise. Just as I started to turn I got hit—

(indicates back of head)

. . . I remember falling to my knees—and . . . that's all.

(rubs face with towel)

MULVEY

Listen, Niles—you came very close to not waking up at all. The party that killed Jean Dexter tried the same business on you. Who was it?

NILES

(resentfully)

How on earth would I know?

MULVEY

If you're afraid, I'll guarantee you police protection.

NILES

If I knew, I'd tell you. I'm not a fool. Do you think I enjoyed this?

(rubs face)

MULVEY

Got any guess who it was?

NILES

It must've been a burglar. Came in by the fire escape, I suppose.

MULVEY
A burglar? Maybe he stole something.
Niles stiffens. He gets up as quickly as his condition permits, goes to divan, searches anxiously through the suitcase and among the things strewn about. It is clear that he is searching for something he can't find. Then he stops, turns.

MULVEY
He got it—didn't he?

NILES
No . . . no . . . there's nothing missing.
(quickly)
I don't have any valuables.

MULVEY
What were you just looking for so hard—your B.V.D.'s.?

NILES
I thought . . . I forgot this was in my pocket.
He takes out a jewel-studded cigarette lighter.

NILES
(continuing)
It's my one valuable—I only got it two weeks ago—it's expensive.

MULVEY
Jimmy—
Halloran takes it from Niles, pulls Department list of stolen jewelry out of his pocket. Ruth watches with terrified apprehension. Niles seems bewildered.

NILES
What are you doing?
Silence. Halloran is busy with the list.

NILES
(continuing)
Why'd you come down here anyway?
Silence.

NILES
(continuing excitedly)

You want to know something, Lieutenant? You're going to
have a lawsuit on your hands. You can—

HALLORAN
(interrupting)
Forrest C. Broughton, 85 West 68th Street, reported the loss
of this cigarette lighter three weeks ago. Night robbery.
Silence. All look at Niles. Ruth's face is sick.

NILES
What kind of a deal is this?

MULVEY
You tell us.

NILES
If you think I'm a thief, you're crazy.
(to Ruth)
Honey, this is the craziest thing I ever heard of.

RUTH
(tortured at asking)
Sweetheart—this is a terrible thing to ask you right now,
but . . . my engagement ring—where'd you buy it?

NILES
(stunned)
What?

RUTH
Robert, darling—please—where'd you buy it?

NILES
It was from a private party.

RUTH
(relieved)
Who, Robert?

NILES
I can't tell you.

RUTH
Please, sweetheart, you must. Don't you understand?—

MULVEY
(sharply; interrupting)
Where'd you get the cigarette case you sold this morning?

ROBERT
(pressed to wall)
What?

MULVEY
How'd you get this cigarette lighter?

Silence.

RUTH
(hysterically)
Robert—tell them—please, tell them.

MULVEY
Why'd you buy a plane ticket for Mexico City?

NILES
(stunned)
Why, I—

RUTH
What ticket? When?

MULVEY
He was supposed to leave tomorrow noon.

RUTH
Is that true?

Silence.

RUTH
Robert—is it true?

NILES
A business trip—

RUTH
We had lunch today. Why didn't you . . .?

NILES
(interrupting)
Something came up this afternoon.

MULVEY

You're lying—you bought the ticket in the morning.
Niles suddenly straightens, looks at Mulvey coolly.

NILES

You've got the wrong man if you think I stole those things.
I wouldn't steal a piece of bread if I was starving. That isn't
how I was brought up. I come from a decent family.

MULVEY

Congratulations.

NILES

I got this lighter as a present. You can't send me to prison
for that.

MULVEY

Who gave it to you?

NILES
(with quiet triumph)
Jean Dexter. Now you prove she didn't.

MULVEY

And the cigarette case you sold this morning?

NILES

The same.

RUTH

And my engagement ring?

NILES

Sure—Jean gave me that too.

RUTH

My *engagement* ring?

NILES

You heard me.

RUTH
(approaching him)
No, no, darling, don't say a thing like that. That would be
horrible. And I know it's a lie. You hardly knew Jean—

NILES
(coolly)
I'm sorry, Ruth.

RUTH
I don't believe you. Robert, I love you. I'll marry you now—
tonight. But say you're lying about Jean. If you're a thief, I'll
stand by you, I'll—

NILES
(hysterically)
And go to prison? In a pig's eye I will. Those things were
presents—presents—your ring was a present—from Jean—

RUTH
Robert—
He is silent.

RUTH
You're lying.
(hits him hard)
You're lying.
(hits him)
You're lying.
(hits him)
Sobbing hysterically, Ruth continues to hit him. Niles backs off, raising his hands against her blows. Halloran catches hold of Ruth, re-
strains her. She breaks down in sobs.

MULVEY
Niles—you're under arrest.

NILES
(hysterically)
Arrest me all you like. But try to prove something against
me—try it—just try it.

DISSOLVE TO:

EXT THE STREET IN FRONT OF THE POLICE STATION DAY
Girls are jumping rope. Two girls swing the rope, a third jumps. One
of the girls recites in a loud voice.

                        GIRL
        Mother, Mother, I am ill;
        Call the doctor over the hill;

EXT   MULVEY   DAY
looking down from third story window with a smile.

                    GIRL'S VOICE
            In came the doctor, in came the nurse,
            In came the lady with the alligator purse—

EXT   CHILDREN   DAY
from Mulvey's POV

                        GIRL
            I don't want the doctor,
            I don't want the nurse.
            I don't want the lady
            with the alligator purse.

                    HALLORAN'S VOICE
        Dan . . .

INT   MULVEY'S OFFICE   DAY
Mulvey turns.

                    HALLORAN
                (hesitantly)
        I'm not sure but I think maybe I've found a connection be-
        tween these jewel robberies and the Dexter murder.

                        MULVEY
                (with interest)
        Oh?
                (shuts window)

                    GIRL'S VOICE
                (from outside—not clear)
        Out went the doctor,
        Out went the nurse,
        Out went the lady
        With the alligator purse.

HALLORAN

Have you read this autopsy report on Peter Backalis?
(indicates paper)

MULVEY

Not yet.

HALLORAN

Yesterday morning some kids swimming in the East River
found a body. Medical examiner says he died of drowning—
had a head injury and was full of whiskey. His verdict is
accidental death.

MULVEY

Well? . . .

HALLORAN

But look at this: Jean Dexter died between one and two A.M.
Monday morning. This guy Backalis died between three
and six A.M. the same morning.

MULVEY

Show me that it's more than a coincidence.

HALLORAN

I can't show you, Dan . . . but the man had a record. He
served two years in Sing Sing for stealing *jewelry*.

MULVEY

(smiling)
Now look—Niles and Dexter were dealing in stolen jewelry,
sure. But it was society stuff. What does Backalis's record
show?

HALLORAN

(chagrined)
I didn't think of that. It was small time—a pawn shop robbery in Queens.

MULVEY

Y'see? I'm afraid these two cases are miles apart. If we drag
every petty jewelry thief into this, we'll go crazy.
(looks at him)
But you're not convinced, are you?

HALLORAN

I don't know, Dan. Trouble is, where are we on the Dexter case?

MULVEY

This morning I sent out photos of Niles and Dexter to every Police Department on the East Coast. They'll check all jewelers.

HALLORAN

Where can that lead?

MULVEY

That's how you run a case, lad . . . from step to step.

HALLORAN

Do me a favor, Dan. Let me waste some time on this Backalis angle.

A pause. Mulvey thinks it over.

MULVEY

Okay, lad. Phone in once a day.

HALLORAN

Thanks.

MULVEY

By the way . . .

Halloran pauses.

MULVEY

(softly)

This is only the third day now on the Dexter murder. The Department never calls a case unsolved in less than twenty years. Don't get impatient.

HALLORAN

Good deal. Twenty years from now, I'll put my kid on it.

He leaves, smiling. Mulvey grins.

EXT POLICE HEADQUARTERS	NARRATOR
CENTRE STREET DAY	Button, button, who's got the
People going in and out.	button?

INT   A FILE ROOM   DAY

Halloran waits while a clerk looks in a file. Clerk takes out a card.

CLERK

Backalis's parole officer was Charles Freed. County Courthouse in the Bronx.

Halloran turns, starts out.

EXT BRONX COUNTY COURTHOUSE DAY
as Halloran enters.

INT AN OFFICE BRONX COUNTY COURTHOUSE DAY
Halloran is sitting with a parole officer, CHARLES FREED, a man of
fifty, bald.

HALLORAN

Well, tell me this, Mr. Freed . . . Do you think Backalis
could get so drunk he'd fall down on a pier, hurt himself
and topple into the river?

FREED

(thinking)
I doubt it. He seemed like one of those steady, all-day drink-
ers—always with a load on, but never wobbly.

HALLORAN

Who was the arresting officer?

FREED

Patrolman Albert Hicks—Queensboro Precinct Station, Long
Island City.

HALLORAN

Right on my doorstep! What do you know. . . .

EXT BRIDGE ABOVE LONG ISLAND CITY RAILROAD YARDS
NIGHT

EXT HALLORAN AND HICKS NIGHT
a Negro patrolman.

HALLORAN

About two and a half years ago you arrested Peter Backalis
on a pawnshop entry.

HICKS

That's right.

HALLORAN

Did he do that job alone?

HICKS

No—there was another guy with him—a feller he called Willie.

HALLORAN

What happened to him?

HICKS

He got away by the neatest trick I've ever seen. I nailed Backalis in the back alley. He yelled "Beat it, Willie," and this other customer throws a chair through a plate glass window—dives right after it—and comes up on his feet like an acrobat. Then he's off like a streak.

HALLORAN

How was this fellow built?

HICKS

Big—like an all-American fullback . . . And listen . . . something funny about him. One of the things the owner reported missing was a harmonica. Now there's no resale value in a thing like that. So I always figured he must've liked to play one.

HALLORAN

Maybe you're right. Much obliged.

INT MULVEY'S BEDROOM NIGHT
Mulvey is on telephone. Light is on. A newspaper on bed indicates he's been reading.

MULVEY
(thoughtfully)
A big man who's an acrobat, eh?
(listens)
Jimmy, I don't know where you're going—but I'm gonna start in and help you. I'm giving you Fowler and Constentino, starting tomorrow morning.
(listens)
Right.

INT HALLORAN LIVING ROOM NIGHT

HALLORAN
(at phone)

'Bye, Dan.
Hangs up, yawns. Starts taking off coat.

EXT TIMES SQUARE DAY	NARRATOR
Halloran, Constentino, Fowler are talking	His name is Willie—maybe. He might've been a professional ac-
The three men separate, go in different directions.	robat—maybe. He might be the man we're looking for . . . maybe. Oh, yes—he's a big man. Only half a million big men in New York.

INT   OFFICE   DAY
A bald, thin, acidulous-looking man is talking to Halloran. On wall, autographed photos from vaudeville actors.

                    BOOKING AGENT
. . . Not that I can remember. I been booking vaudeville acts, circus acts, night club acts, for thirty years. Lot of queer eggs among 'em—but a acrobat who played the harmonica? That queer I never saw one.

                    HALLORAN
          (disappointed)
Okay . . . thanks.

INT   STILLMAN'S GYMNASIUM   DAY
Men are working out in ring. Off to one side Fowler talks to Stillman.

                    STILLMAN
A harmonica player? No, sir, brother. A character like that I wouldn't even let work out here.
                                        DISSOLVE TO:

INT   A GYMNASIUM WHERE WRESTLERS PRACTICE   DAY
Two wrestlers are intertwined on a mat; both are heavyweights. A trainer and another wrestler are watching. Constentino comes in.

                    CONSTENTINO
Who runs this joint?

                    TRAINER
I do. What do you want?

                    CONSTENTINO
          (showing badge)

Police.

Instantly the two wrestlers freeze in an intertwined position, look up.

> CONSTENTINO
>
> Any of you guys ever know a wrestler who liked to play the harmonica?

> TRAINER
>
> Sure—Willie the harmonica player—Willie Garza—I teached him to wrastle.

One of the wrestlers on mat looks up.

> WRESTLER
>
> You didn't teach him so good. I kokalized him in Scranton five years ago.

> CONSTENTINO
>
> Where's he now?

> TRAINER
>
> Don't know—don't care. He borrowed thirty-eight bucks from me once, never paid it back. A lousola.

> CONSTENTINO
>
> Where'd he used to live?

> TRAINER
>
> Don't know.

> WRESTLER
>
> In Staten Island—with his brother.

> CONSTENTINO
>
> What's his brother's name?

> WRESTLER
>
> Garza. All brothers got the same names.

> CONSTENTINO
>
> I mean his first name.

> WRESTLER
>
> I dunno.

> CONSTENTINO
>
> Okay.
>   (leaves)

DISSOLVE TO:

EXT TOP FLOOR OF A BUILDING UNDER CONSTRUCTION DAY
Halloran, Constentino and a foreman are walking up to a welder at
work.

> FOREMAN
> Hey, Garza—Eddie—

Garza turns.

> FOREMAN
> These guys are police—want to talk to you.

> EDDIE GARZA
> (apprehensive)
> Something happen to my wife?

> HALLORAN
> Oh, no. We just saw her. That's how we found out where
> you work.

> EDDIE GARZA
> What is it?

> HALLORAN
> We're looking for your brother—Willie.

> EDDIE GARZA
> Me an' my brother Willie ain't got nothing to do with each
> other. He's no good.

> CONSTENTINO
> When'd you see him last?

> EDDIE GARZA
> Three months ago about.
> (laughs)
> Tried to sell me a diamond ring for my wife. I told him to
> go blow.

> HALLORAN
> Any idea at all where he lives?

> EDDIE GARZA
> He had a room somewhere around the Williamsburg Bridge.
> That's all I know.

CONSTENTINO
You got a picture of him?

EDDIE GARZA
No. But when he was wrestlin' the newspapers printed his mug a few times.

HALLORAN
Okay.
They start off.

EDDIE GARZA
If you send him up, do me a favor . . . throw the keys away.

EXT   EAST SIDE TENEMENTS OVERSHADOWED BY THE WILLIAMSBURG BRIDGE   NIGHT

INT   CAFETERIA   NIGHT
Halloran, Fowler, and Constentino at a table. They have finished eating and each is studying a sectional map of the district.

HALLORAN
The first guy to get a lead report to Mulvey.
The others nod. Halloran gives them each a photo of Garza, a wrestling pose, full-length.

EXT   A STREET CORNER
NIGHT
Fowler goes up to an old woman pretzel seller. He shows her the photo.

NARRATOR
Lady—did you ever see a man looked like this?

Woman shakes her head.

EXT   A CHEAP MOVIE THEATER   NIGHT
Constentino is showing photo to ticket taker. He shakes head.

NARRATOR
Hey, buddy, ever see a man looked like this?

INT   A CHEAP BAR   NIGHT
Halloran is showing photo to a bartender.

How's your memory for faces, Mac?

INT   PRECINCT HEADQUARTERS   NIGHT
A large squad of patrolmen is

Here's a chance to get a promotion, men. Just spot this guy out

lined up, ready to go out on its
beat. Fowler is showing them the
photo.

EXT   TENEMENTS, WILLIAMS-
BURG BRIDGE   DAY

EXT   EAST SIDE STREET   NIGHT
Constentino comes up to
pushcart peddler, shows him
photo.

INT   TAILOR SHOP   DAY
as Fowler shows photo to a
worker at a steaming pressing
machine.

of half a million people.

Another day . . .

. . . work day . . .

. . . hot summer day . . .

INT   DRUG STORE   PHONE BOOTH   DAY
Halloran has the receiver to his ear, is waiting. While he waits, he
blocks out a street on his sectional map. A whole series of streets
have already been blocked out. He looks tired, drawn.

                    HALLORAN
            (into phone)
        Hello, Dan . . . Jimmy.
            (voice is tired)
        No . . . nothing so far.
            (listens)
        Sure, I'll keep going. What's doing at your end?

INT   MULVEY'S OFFICE   DAY
In the office are Mulvey, Niles, Miller, Perelli.

                    MULVEY
            (into phone)
        Doing fine here. I'm talking to that clean-cut young Ameri-
        can beauty again.
            (listens)
        I think he's going to tell us something this morning.
            (Niles fidgets)
        Okay—report in.
            (hangs up)

                    NILES
        I've told you everything I know.

> MULVEY
> (pleasantly)
> No, you haven't, sonny.
> (rises, starts for door
> But you will.

Mulvey opens door.

> MULVEY
> (continuing)
> Come in, Mr. McCormick.

Niles jumps to his feet as a stout, middle-aged man enters.

> MULVEY
> (continuing)
> (to McCormick)
> Recognize this man?

> McCORMICK
> I certainly do.

With surprising agility, McCormick lunges at Niles and punches him in the jaw. Niles crumples under the weight of the blow and sags to the floor. Perelli grabs McCormick.

> MULVEY
> Sit down. If there's any more of that, you'll get yourself in trouble.
> (to Niles)
> Getting quite a slapping around these days, aren't you?

McCormick sits. Niles has gotten up. He holds a handkerchief to his mouth.

> McCORMICK
> I came all the way down from Boston to do that. That smooth-talking crook came to me with an introduction I had to honor. He gave me a song and dance—his sister was terribly sick—needed an operation—he was trying to sell her jewels. I paid him over three thousand dollars. Now it turns out to be stolen property.

> NILES
> Are you paying him to say that, Mulvey? You still can't prove anything.

McCORMICK

I can.
>(pulls a letter from his pocket)

I run my business with great care. This is the letter of introduction he brought with him.

Niles stiffens. Mulvey takes the letter, looks at it.

MULVEY

Dr. Lawrence Stoneman!

McCORMICK

He treated my mother some years ago. I *had* to honor his
letter.

Mulvey's eyes are now riveted on Niles.

MULVEY

Will you wait outside, Mr. McCormick?

McCormick goes out. Perelli shuts door. Silence. Mulvey, Perelli and
Miller are all staring at Niles.

MULVEY

How do you get a letter of introduction from a man like
Stoneman?
    (silence)
You're going to the penitentiary, Niles.
    (pause)
But from now on in, the length of your sentence depends on
you.
    (pause)
Stealing jewelry is one thing—but murder is different.

NILES

    (stubbornly)
You know I didn't kill her! I was at the Trinidad Club. There
are witnesses.

MULVEY

Then who did kill her?

NILES

I don't know.

MULVEY

Who's Henderson?

NILES

I don't know.

MULVEY

Listen, young fellow . . . you'll get five years for stealing
jewelry. But you'll get another ten years for obstructing jus-
tice . . . and ten years more for being an accessory after the
fact. Now that's the way it is, sonny boy . . . and you know
I'm not bluffing.
    (jumping up)
Who's Henderson? Who's Henderson?

NILES

Stoneman . . . He's Dr. Stoneman.
Mulvey looks at the others in triumph.

EXT   EAST SIDE STREET   DAY
A street sign: RIVINGTON STREET

CAMERA MOVES DOWN to take in Halloran, looking at sign. He crosses a bit wearily to a corner soda fountain that opens onto the street. He leans on counter, blocks off another street on his sectional map. The proprietress moves over, a middle-aged woman, stout, workworn, wearing glasses.

                    HALLORAN
          You got any cold root beer?

                    PROPRIETRESS
          Like ice.
As woman fills order, Halloran holds out a photo of Garza.

                    HALLORAN
          Ever see this man?
The proprietress takes the photo, looks at it.

                    PROPRIETRESS
          He's a box fighter?

                    HALLORAN
          A wrestler.

                    PROPRIETRESS
               (laughs)
          Boxing, wrestling, what do I know?
               (returns photo)
          Five cents, pleez.
Halloran takes out coin, gives it to her. The woman's brow furrows suddenly. She picks up photo again.

                    PROPRIETRESS
          Pleez.
She studies photo, puts her hand across it to block out all but the face.

                    PROPRIETRESS
               (continuing)
          He's a feller likes to play the whatchamacallit?
She gestures playing the harmonica. Halloran almost jumps out of his skin.

                    HALLORAN
          The harmonica! Yes!

                    PROPRIETRESS
          Sure, I know him—Willie!

> HALLORAN

Where does he live?

> PROPRIETRESS

This street someplace.

> HALLORAN

What house?

> PROPRIETRESS

Down the street someplace. I dunno.

Halloran walks quickly around counter into store. He crosses to phone, dials. The proprietress comes up to him with an anxious look.

> PROPRIETRESS

Who you, Mista?

Halloran doesn't answer.

> PROPRIETRESS
> (continuing)

You from a collection agency, maybe?

> HALLORAN
> (into phone)

Ben? This is Jimmy. Dan there?
> (listens)

When he gets back, tell him I've located Garza. Somewhere on Rivington between Delancey and Essex. 'Bye.

He hangs up. The proprietress timidly plucks his sleeve.

> PROPRIETRESS

Pleez, Mista—by me Willie's a nice feller. A man likes kids, he's nice. Any little kid asks him, Willie plays his whatcha-macallit. I don't want I should make trouble for him.

> HALLORAN
> (showing badge)

Don't worry, lady.

Halloran leaves.

> PROPRIETRESS
> (calling after him)

You don't want your root beer, Mista?

EXT SQUIBB BUILDING DAY

Mulvey, Perelli, Niles and another detective are on their way into the building. A police sedan is parked at curb.

EXT   RIVINGTON STREET   DAY

Halloran walks up to a thin, stooped woman who is sitting on steps with a baby in her arms

> HALLORAN
>
> Does Willie Garza live here?
> (shows photo)

The woman looks at photo, speaks with an Italian accent.

> WOMAN
>
> He'sa not live here.

> HALLORAN
>
> You sure?

> WOMAN
>
> My hoosband he'sa janitor. I'm positive.

> HALLORAN
>
> Thanks.

He moves on.

INT   CORRIDOR OF SQUIBB BUILDING   DAY

Mulvey and his party are walking along a series of offices. The windows are marked "Dr. Stoneman." An arrow points to an entrance further on. Mulvey gestures to a detective we haven't seen before, to cover Stoneman's last door.

> MULVEY
>
> Nobody gets by you.

The party goes on, enters reception room. There are three patients waiting. Mulvey goes up to nurse, shows badge, whispers.

> MULVEY
>
> I'm Lieutenant Mulvey of the Police Department. Is Dr. Stoneman in?

> NURSE
>
> He's with a patient.

> MULVEY
>
> I want you to do exactly as I say, Miss. Tell the patients who are waiting that they have to leave.

NURSE

But—

MULVEY

Do what I say, Miss—

The nurse looks at him, rises.

EXT RIVINGTON STREET DAY

Halloran walks up to two little girls who are playing jacks on the steps of a house.

HALLORAN

Do you kids know a man who lives on this street by the name of Willie Garza?

The girls look at each other blankly.

HALLORAN

(continuing)

He plays the harmonica.

One of the girls smiles.

GIRL

I know him. Willie.

HALLORAN

Where does he live?

GIRL

Across the street—corner house, I think—or the next one.

HALLORAN

Good girl.

Leaves.

INT STONEMAN'S OFFICE DAY

The nurse is just closing the door on the last of the patients. She turns on Mulvey angrily.

NURSE

This is really unheard of.

MULVEY

I know, M'am.

(to Niles)

Sit there. Don't say anything.

He points to a chair directly opposite the entrance to Stoneman's office. Niles obeys.

> MULVEY
> (continuing—to nurse)
> Tell Dr. Stoneman somebody out here has to see him. Tell him to leave his patient and come out right now. And don't tell him anything else.

> NURSE
> (almost weeping)
> I'll lose my job over this.
> (picks up phone—waits)
> Doctor—
> (beginning to sob)
> There's someone here. He has to see you. You have to come right out.
> (listens—sobbing)
> You must, doctor, right now, you must.

The nurse hangs up with a bang and bursts into tears. Mulvey and Perelli move quickly into a small recess in the office behind the nurse's desk. The door opens. Stoneman comes out, looking very irritated. He stops dead when he sees Niles.

> STONEMAN
> (icily)
> What are you doing here?

Niles says nothing. He is looking at Mulvey. Stoneman turns.

> STONEMAN
> Who are you?

> MULVEY
> Lieutenant Mulvey of the Homicide Squad. Do you go by the name of Henderson?

Slowly Stoneman seems to cave in.

> STONEMAN
> Yes.

> MULVEY
> You're under arrest for the murder of Jean Dexter.

STONEMAN
(with a low cry of horror)
No! I couldn't do anything like that.
(swinging on Niles)
If anyone did it, it was him!
(buries head in hands, sinks into chair)
Finished—I'm finished now. . . .

MULVEY
What was your relationship to Niles and Dexter?

STONEMAN
(with a low cry of shame, ripped from his gut)
A lamb led to slaughter! An idiot robbed of self-respect, of
manhood, of decency!
(half sobs; in a low voice)
I loved that girl the way a sick man loves alcohol or a nar-
cotic. There was nothing right about it or good about it, only
a sick hunger. I saw her a year ago in that dress shop. And
from then on I was drunk with her, lost.
(turns on Niles)
For six months now I've known they've been using me. I
was their tipster—me—Stoneman.

MULVEY
What do you mean?

STONEMAN
It wasn't enough I poured money out on her. Jean was
twisted inside, too, like me.
(with a bewildered cry)
What does life do to people that it can set up such unnatural
hungers in them—me for a woman like her—and she for
money?
(gestures)
She was a common thief.
(looking at Niles)
Both of them. They used my social connections. My wife is
a partygiver. Jean'd find out from me who was to be there.
And it was only after months that I realized that when

someone came to my house, his apartment was robbed the same night.

MULVEY

Why didn't you go to the police?
Stoneman gestures despairingly.

STONEMAN

Why doesn't a drug addict stop taking drugs? She kept promising me each time was the last. I believed her because I wanted to believe her. I believed her because I was afraid to go to the police—afraid of the scandal. You can read about sick people like me in medical literature. Here I am. Look at me. I'm contemptible.

MULVEY

Did you arrange the robbery of your own apartment?

STONEMAN

Yes. I even came to that. I was frightened and I had to wallow in my own filth.
        (jumps up)
Oh, I'm so glad you came. Prison is much better than insanity—and I'm half mad already.
        (with a groan)
Oh, Stoneman, what have you become?

MULVEY

What proof have you that you didn't kill Dexter?

STONEMAN

Proof?
        (rubs hand over brow)
I was someplace else—Miss Owen—my date book—yes—a birthday party—at the Broughtons.

MULVEY

Will you testify in court that Niles and Dexter did these robberies?

NILES

        (with a cry)
I never did!

MULVEY

Shut up.

STONEMAN

No, they were the fixers, the smart ones. They used *me* one
way—they hired other men for the actual robberies.

MULVEY

Who?

Stoneman rubs hand over brow.

STONEMAN

I don't know.
  (to Nurse)
Miss Owen—my practice—Oh, don't cry . . .
  (groans)
You'll call Dr. Grenard.
  (to Mulvey—beseechingly)
Only don't let me have to see anyone . . . Not my wife . . .
no friends . . . no lawyer. Just lock me up and hide me away.
  (suddenly stiffens, looks around)
Me? Stoneman?
  (with a cry)
It's impossible. I won't have it.

Suddenly, with a distorted face, he hurtles himself across the room
toward the large window that faces the city.

STONEMAN

  (continuing)
I won't have it!

MULVEY

Grab him!

Perelli and another officer make a lunge for Stoneman, but Niles is
closest. Niles leaps for the doctor, tackling him just as the doctor hits
the window pane. The glass is shattered, but the doctor—a pitiful and
forlorn figure—is pulled back into a chair. He puts his head in his
hands, sobs brokenly.

MULVEY

  (quietly)
I don't know much about medicine, doctor—but I'm pretty
sure that's one prescription never cured anything.

> (to Niles)
> Thanks, Niles. And as long as you finally made up your
> mind to cooperate, why not go all the way? You're not stu-
> pid. You're hooked now, and you know it. So why not spill
> the rest?
> (quiet intensity)
> Who did the jobs for you? Who was it?

There is a strained silence for a moment. Then—

NILES

> Willie Garza. He and Backalis. They wanted more of a cut
> from the robberies. Garza killed Jean; then later that night
> he killed Backalis.
> (leans forward)
> I loved Jean. I didn't have anything to do with it. It was
> Garza . . . Garza . . . Garza . . .

INT   TENEMENT HOUSE   DAY

Halloran is walking up a flight of stairs. There is the SOUND of someone practicing scales on the violin. He reaches the landing, crosses to
a door in the search for a number. As he leaves door we hear a voice
from within:

MAN'S VOICE

> You must practice more—practice—

Halloran crosses to another door, listens, knocks. A deep, hearty voice
answers.

GARZA'S VOICE

> Come on in!

Halloran enters.

INT   GARZA'S APARTMENT   DAY

A cheaply furnished, two-room apartment. Garza is lying on the floor
doing a wrestler's bridge by way of exercise. He is a very muscular
man in fine condition. At the moment he is wearing only sneakers
and tights. He swivels his head a little to one side to see who has come
in, but he doesn't change his position. He has a face that combines
toughness and shrewdness; he appears to be about thirty-five.

Throughout the scene we faintly hear the practicing of violin scales
from the other apartment.

GARZA

(genially)

I thought it was the janitor for the rent. Who're you? Don't mind me. Just having a little work-out.

As Garza says this, he swivels at the neck and turns his body and feet and head over, so that he is face down. His torso and legs have not touched the floor in the course of the stunt.

HALLORAN

My name's Hawkey—I work up at Bellevue hospital. Are you Willie Garza?

GARZA

That's me. Ever see me wrestle? I wasn't so bad.

(swivels body over)

HALLORAN

No, I never did. There's a patient at the hospital gave me your address—asked me to see you.

GARZA

Yeah. Who?

He works his body up and down, exercising his abdominal muscles.

HALLORAN

Backalis his name is.

Garza seems to pause for a second. Then he swivels over, face down.

GARZA

Pete? What's he doin' in the hospital?

HALLORAN

He almost got drowned. Fell in the river when he was plastered. Some guy on a tug boat fished him out.

GARZA

You don't say?

(laughs)

Oh, that Pete. Can't let the booze alone. So what does he want from me?

(swivels around)

HALLORAN

He says he wants to see you.

GARZA

You know what he wants?

(lowers body to floor)

He wants money.

Now Garza raises legs high, then does a snap up. He lands feet on floor.

GARZA

(continuing)

Some condition I'm in, hey, brother?

(crosses to a chair for a towel)

Don't smoke, don't drink.

(rubs body with towel)

So Pete wants money again?

(shakes head . . . coming closer)

You know what you can tell him, buddy?

Now, from several feet away, Garza suddenly leaps like a cat. The heavy Turkish towel goes over Halloran's head. Garza grabs him, trips him, slams him savagely to the floor. In another second his legs have scissored over Halloran's and one hand holds Halloran's arm in a hammer lock.

GARZA

(continuing)

Lay still or I'll snap your arm like a wishbone.

His free hand explores Halloran's pockets, then finds the gun around his hip. He removes gun, presses it into Halloran's ribs. Then he disengages himself, gets up. Halloran slowly rises.

GARZA

(continuing)

Copper, ain't you?

HALLORAN

Yeah.

GARZA

Just because I'm big, everybody thinks I'm dumb. I'm not dumb, I'm smart. Now how did I know you were a copper? Because *nobody* knows where I live—not even Pete Backalis.

HALLORAN

If you're smart, you'll come down to headquarters with me.

GARZA

Ha-ha—that wouldn't be smart. You know why? 'Cause
Backalis ain't in Bellevue, he's in the morgue.
(dangerously)
Turn around.

HALLORAN

(obeying)
Don't be a fool.

From now on CAMERA becomes Halloran's eyes. We see only what
Halloran sees—a stretch of dirty wallpaper and a cheap reproduction
of da Vinci's *Last Supper* thumbtacked to the wall.

GARZA'S VOICE

I'll prove I'm smart, copper. You know how? You're scared
right now I'm gonna rub you out. But I ain't—'cause I'm
smart. Ain't nobody can prove I rubbed out Backalis. So
why should I knock you off? Rub out a cop an' you'll really
get the chair. All I need to do is put you to sleep. Then I'm
off. Try an' find me. This is a great big, beautiful city. Just
try an' find me.

There is a grunt from Garza, the sound of a fist striking flesh. The picture of the *Last Supper* suddenly blurs violently as the CAMERA shakes. Then the CAMERA starts tilting towards the floor.

GARZA'S VOICE

That was a rabbit punch, Copper. It's strictly illegal.

Again there is the crack of a fist. The screen goes black.

INT STONEMAN'S RECEPTION ROOM DAY

Mulvey is at the phone. Perelli, Niles, and Dr. Stoneman are on their way out of the office.

MULVEY

(into phone)

Yeah, he signed it. Wait a minute, Ben.

(to Perelli; calling)

Keep Niles away from the newspaper men.

(into phone)

And listen, Ben—when Halloran calls in—or Fowler or Constentino—tell 'em that Willie Garza may be the gimmick in this case. So—

(stops talking, listens; suddenly snaps up)

When did Halloran call in? Was he alone?

(listens)

Now get this—send out an emergency! Rush every available squad car. Block off the street. Surround it.

He hangs up. Jumps to his feet. Starts running out.

INT POLICE HEADQUARTERS RADIO ROOM DAY

A patrolman is crossing quickly from plotting table to radio operator at microphone. He gives operator a paper.

PATROLMAN

Emergency!

OPERATOR

(into microphone)

Emergency . . . All squad cars on the East Side of 14th Street to the Williamsburg Bridge, from 1st Street to 5th Avenue, proceed immediately to Rivington Street between Essex and Delancey. Block off and surround both sides of the street. Institute immediate house-to-house search for—

INT SQUAD CAR (PROCESS) DAY
swinging around in middle of street and then racing down Third
Avenue with siren screaming. The operator's voice continued.

                    OPERATOR'S VOICE
          —two men—Detective James Halloran and William Garza.
          Halloran is twenty-eight years old . . .

INT GARZA'S ROOM DAY
Halloran is stretched out near wall, unconscious. Garza has put on a
sport shirt and trousers. He still wears sneakers. The butts of two
guns show above his belt, at waist line. He is stuffing four small
chamois bags into both side pockets. He grabs up a sports jacket, puts
it on. He opens a cupboard drawer, takes out a harmonica, puts it in
a side pocket of his jacket. Then he goes out. The instant the door
shuts Halloran sits up. The sudden movement makes him gasp with
nausea. He remains still a second, then slowly pushes himself to his
feet. On wobbly legs he starts for the door.

INT STAIRCASE DAY
Garza is coming rapidly downstairs.

INT GARZA DAY
as seen down stairwell by Halloran. Halloran starts down slowly, on
shaky legs, holding to banister.

INT FIRST-FLOOR LANDING DAY
CAMERA IS SHOOTING UP as Garza comes down.

SOUND: A police siren; a second, a third, approaching. Garza
freezes for a second, then races down the last steps to the landing. He runs to the front door, flattens himself against the wall
and glances out through the glass.

EXT TENEMENT ACROSS FROM GARZA DAY

CAMERA IS GARZA'S EYES.
A black police sedan is moving slowly along. A detective is questioning the two little girls who are playing jacks. One of them points toward Garza's tenement. CAMERA SWINGS to show cops and
plainclothesmen leaping out of cars. CAMERA SWINGS other way to
show Mulvey and others starting across street at a run.

INT HALLWAY DAY

Garza turns, starts running toward back of hall. As he does so, he sees Halloran coming down last flight of stairs. Garza pulls out a gun but keeps running. Halloran hurtles down, swings out and around, trips and falls. At the same instant of his falling, Garza has swung around while opening the back door. He fires; the bullet shatters the window of the front door. Garza leaps outside. Halloran gets up, runs towards the back door. The front door swings open. Mulvey rushes in, gun in hand.

                         MULVEY
                    (yelling)
          Jimmy!

                         HALLORAN
                    (without stopping)
               This way.
Mulvey runs after him.

EXT BACK YARD TENEMENT HOUSE DAY
It is a mass of clotheslines, with wet wash hanging from every line. Garza is about to climb the fence at one end, when he spots Halloran in pursuit. He stops and fires another shot. Halloran falls flat on the pavement; then gets up untouched. He follows Garza over the fence. Mulvey appears at Halloran starts over. He changes course, runs out down a side alley.

EXT ALLEYWAY DAY
On the other side of the fence is a long alleyway, with ash cans and piles of junk in evidence. Garza runs down the alleyway with Halloran still in pursuit. Garza stops and fires again. Halloran drops behind an ash can as the bullet ricochets off it.

EXT END OF ALLEYWAY DAY
Garza climbs another fence, finds himself in back of a butcher store. He dashes into the store, with Halloran following a few seconds later.

INT BUTCHER STORE DAY
as Garza runs through with gun in hand, followed by Halloran. The clerks and customers stare in horror.

EXT STREET IN FRONT OF BUTCHER STORE DAY
This is Delancey Street, a business thoroughfare. Across the street stands the approach to the huge Williamsburg Bridge which crosses

the East River to Brooklyn. The street is crowded with automobiles.
Garza races across. Halloran follows. Coming up behind Halloran is
Qualen, the detective we saw earlier at Stoneman's.

EXT DELANCEY STREET DAY
as Garza disregards traffic and runs across. A truck swerves to escape
hitting him. Another car jams on brakes. A third car crashes into the
second. A traffic cop blows his whistle furiously. Halloran keeps after
Garza. Qualen has caught up with Halloran now. Garza starts up the
stone steps to the footwalk on the bridge. Qualen fires, misses. Garza
turns, fires. Both Qualen and Halloran hurl themselves to sidewalk.
Garza runs. They follow.

EXT STREET DAY
Mulvey, detectives, run up. Traffic is now stationary. Mulvey runs toward cop.

                    MULVEY
              (yelling)
        Hold all bridge traffic.

(to a cop)
Stop traffic on the Brooklyn end.
He runs to a radio car which swings into scene. Jumps in.

EXT BRIDGE FOOTWALK DAY
CAMERA FRAMES the city. Suddenly frame is filled by sweaty,
distorted face of Garza as he climbs onto footwalk. He turns violently.

EXT QUALEN AND HALLORAN DAY
from Garza's angle. Garza fires, Qualen falls back down steps into
Halloran's arms, almost hurling Halloran down. Garza turns, runs.

EXT ENTRANCE TO MANHATTAN SIDE OF BRIDGE DAY
as traffic cop stops all traffic, as instructed by Mulvey.

EXT BROOKLYN SIDE OF BRIDGE DAY
as traffic cop steps away from police call box and starts to stop traffic.

EXT LONG SHOT OF BRIDGE SHOOTING DOWN DAY
showing bridge traffic disappearing. CAMERA picks out running
men: Garza, Halloran, several cops. Then it picks out the squad car in
which Mulvey is. The car races ahead of Garza, then stops. Men tum-
ble out. Garza, seeing himself trapped, breaks for the subway tracks
in order to cross to the other side. As he is climbing the fence, one of
the squad car policemen stops running, kneels, aims a rifle. He shoots.
Garza is hit, knocked over the fence and forward by the impact of the
bullet. He staggers, trips over a rail, falls to his knees, slumps over—
and hits the third rail. There is a shower of sparks, his body leaps
convulsively—then is still.

A siren WAILS, higher and higher. CAMERA TILTS toward buildings
of Manhattan, showing sky above. Siren fades out.

EXT SKY NIGHT MOON RID-ING THROUGH FAST CLOUDS.	NARRATOR It's two o'clock in the morning now . . .
EXT ROCKEFELLER CENTER NIGHT	This is the city . . .
EXT BROADWAY AND TIMES SQUARE NIGHT	. . . these are the lights . . .

EXT A NIGHTCLUB NIGHT
A couple stepping into a taxicab.
The two are young, handsome.
The girl is laughing, her face ex-
cited, alive, joyous.

EXT NEWSBOYS NIGHT
getting newspapers from truck in
front of Times Building.

EXT STREET CLEANER NIGHT
sweeping up newspapers.

EXT HALLORAN AND WIFE
NIGHT
standing on a subway platform.
He looks down. Between the
tracks is a newspaper with a picture of Jean Dexter. A train
comes in, the rush of wind blows
away the paper. Halloran puts his
arm around his wife.

INT RUTH YOUNG NIGHT
Riverside Drive apartment. She is
gazing out of her bedroom window, at the Hudson flowing in
moonlight. Her face is sombre.
She is in a dressing robe.

EXT THE BATORYS NIGHT
Mrs. Batory is rocking slowly on
the porch of a small frame house.
Her face is impassive. Mr. Batory
lies on a couch behind her. His
face is in shadow.

EXT PRESBYTERIAN HOSPI-
TAL—168TH STREET NIGHT

. . . that a child born to the name
of Batory hungered for . . . Her
passion has been played out now
. . .

. . . her name, her face, her his-
tory, were worth five cents a day
for six days . . .

. . . and tomorrow will be sold
by the bale . . .

She is not quite forgotten, however . . .

. . . not altogether . . .

. . . not entirely . . .

NARRATOR
. . . and now there is violence
once again in the city . . .

INT DELIVERY ROOM NIGHT
Doctor, nurses—around delivery
table

. . . but of another sort.

INT DOCTOR NIGHT
walks away from table with new-
born baby.

. . . naked and innocent he
comes into this world . . .

INT DOCTOR NIGHT
holds baby upside down by feet,
slaps its buttocks sharply. Baby
wails.

. . . comes to meet the city . . .
naked into a naked city . . .

INT NURSE NIGHT
takes baby from doctor, carries it
to basket. Baby is wailing.

What will he be at twenty?

INT MOTHER'S FACE NIGHT
Quiet, tired.

What will her boy be . . .

INT NILES NIGHT
on a cot in a cell, staring up at
ceiling.

who was born at two o'clock in
the morning . . .

EXT TREES IN CENTRAL PARK
NIGHT

. . . on a hot summer night . . .

EXT MULVEY NIGHT
sitting with his back to a tree,
smoking, looking up at sky

. . . at the time of a shooting star?

EXT SKY NIGHT
A star is falling.

FADE OUT

T H E   E N D

Afterword: The Anatomy of a Hit
By Malvin Wald

Just as in baseball, the chief aim of almost everyone in show business is to score a hit. *Webster's New Collegiate Dictionary* defines a hit as something that is "conspicuously successful" or "a stroke of luck."

The Naked City was a solid hit. In 1948 the British Film Academy nominated it for the award as the best film of the year, along with such classics as Olivier's *Hamlet* (the winner), Rossellini's *Paisan*, and Carol Reed's *The Fallen Idol*. The following year I received an Academy Award nomination from the Hollywood Academy of Motion Picture Arts and Sciences for best-written story; the cinematographer, William Daniels, and the film editor, Paul Weatherwax, won Oscars for their contribution to the film's success.

As the definition suggests, there is also a stroke of luck in any success. *The Naked City* came together at the right time. It was the first film completely shot by a Hollywood producer in New York City using the skyscrapers, streets, and bridges, as well as natural indoor sets of homes and offices. Years later it became the source of a very successful police television series under the same title. *The Naked City* TV series in turn gave birth to a rash of imitations, which can still be seen nightly on the small screen.

Another stroke of luck leading to production of *The Naked City* originated in Brooklyn, the so-called dormitory borough of New York, which was to be the scene of the movie. When I was seventeen years old, I was a junior at Brooklyn College. As an avid reader of the tabloids, two of my journalistic heroes were Mark Hellinger and Walter Winchell, the Butch Cassidy and Sundance Kid of William Randolph Hearst's *Daily Mirror*. Both of these esteemed columnists encouraged readers to mail in contributions. I did so and had some of my adolescent quips printed in both columns. Word spread around my college campus, and I was invited to write a humor column for the school newspaper, *The Pioneer*, a space occupied two years before by a star football player named Irwin Shaw.

135

Shortly after World War II, I found myself as a young Air Force veteran in Hollywood, and I met Mark Hellinger, then a producer at Universal-International Studios, doing his first independent production, Ernest Hemingway's *The Killers*. I recalled my contributions to his column, and Hellinger asked casually, "Did I pay you for them?"

"No," I replied. "But making your column got me started as a writer." My career up to date had been a modest one with screen credits on five long-forgotten films: *Ten Gentlemen From West Point, The Powers Girl, Two in a Taxi, The Underdog,* and *Jive Junction*. My collaborator on *Jive Junction* was a prolific young writer named Irving Wallace, my first friend in Hollywood, who was thrilled to receive his first screen credit.

Hellinger was not satisfied with my reply. He reached for his wallet and offered to pay for those long-ago gags. I steadfastly refused. This irritated Hellinger, famed for his generosity as the fastest check-grabber in the West. "Look," he said, "I'm in debt to you and I don't like that. Here, take some money so I don't have to feel like a heel."

Again I refused. Then he had a bright idea. "Since you're so damned stubborn," he said, "let's make it a business deal. Sell me an old story. Maybe it will be lucky for both of us." He told me how he had just purchased a story from an unknown writer named Patterson and was assigning Richard Brooks to write the screenplay of what turned out to be a splendid film called *Brute Force*. I frustrated Hellinger further by insisting that I wouldn't sell him an unsold story because it probably wasn't very good. But I had a new story approach which excited me very much. This intrigued the old reporter in him, and he questioned me carefully.

I explained that I had just spent almost four years in the Air Force, mostly in the First Motion Picture Unit of the Army Air Forces, where screen personalities such as Ronald Reagan, Alan Ladd, Arthur Kennedy, George Montgomery, Kent Smith, and even Clark Gable were involved in making documentary and training films. Other talents who passed through our unit were directors William Wyler and John Sturges, and writers Norman Krasna, Nedrick Young, Edward Anhalt, Robert Carson, and Jerome Chodorov. One of the most talented of all was a young writer-director of documentaries named Ben Maddow, who was later to write such outstanding films as *Intruder in the Dust* and

The Asphalt Jungle. Ben had worked in New York in documentary films and asked me if I had seen any. I confessed that my training was in playwriting, and I knew little about documentaries.

Ben also discovered a similar ignorance among the other young Army writers, and he organized a series of lunch-hour screenings of the early works of Robert Flaherty, John Grierson, and Joris Ivens. I was greatly moved by the techniques and artistry of Flaherty, considered the "father of the American documentary," and applied his approach in the some thirty documentary and training films I wrote during the war. It was an ironic footnote that in 1948, when *The Naked City* was nominated for an Academy Award, one of my four rivals for the Oscar was the great Robert Flaherty for *The Louisiana Story.*

Hellinger listened patiently to my story about Ben Maddow, Robert Flaherty, and the documentary film and asked what this had to do with Hollywood. "At last," I said triumphantly, "you've hit on the big question. Why doesn't Hollywood leave its sheltered studios and go out in the world and capture the excitement of a city like New York in a feature film, instead of using painted backdrops or street sets on back lots?"

Hellinger considered this carefully and said, "Okay, you may have something there, but where's the story?"

"The story," I replied, "is in the files of the New York Police Department's unsolved cases."

"What has Manhattan Homicide to do with a semi-documentary film?"

I explained that in combining the artistic documentary technique of Flaherty with the commercial product of Hollywood, a safe subject matter should be used—murder, a police story. I admitted that I had never written a crime story before and knew very little about murder detection. However, I pointed out that in the Air Force I knew nothing about flying P-51s, or assembling portable radar sets, or gunnery on the B-29s, or ditching B-17s at sea, or launching guided missiles. But I soon learned about these complex subjects by being assigned to technical advisers who taught me enough to write acceptable scripts. I wanted to do the same thing: have the New York Police Department advise me on scientific crime detection— with the accent on homicide.

Hellinger agreed to finance a one-month research trip to New York

Police Headquarters. He knew William O'Dwyer, the mayor of New York, and he thought he could arrange it. The month spent with those hard-boiled New York City cops was an eye-opener. They did not greet me with open arms. I felt like a criminal suspect as the various detectives eyed me with cold appraisal. They brusquely informed me that they harbored little affection—or respect—for Hollywood screen writers, especially those who wrote murder mysteries based on the books of Dashiell Hammett or Raymond Chandler. In too many fictional movies, police detectives were shown as lazy, comic characters, who wore derbies indoors and spoke out of the side of their mouths like ex-cons. They were portrayed as hopelessly inefficient buffoons and bunglers who could not find a sailor in the Navy Yard without the help of Sam Spade or Philip Marlowe. In most films, they were unable to solve even the simplest murder without the assistance of the wise-cracking private eye and his leggy blonde secretary. And this in the face of the fact that not a single murder had been solved by a private detective in the last quarter-century.

"Look, friend," said one detective, "we don't look upon ourselves as heroes. We're hard-working civil servants trying to support families on $80 or $90 a week. We've paid our dues pounding beats as patrolmen and earned promotions to detectives the hard way."

"We're no glamor boys," pointed out a neatly dressed lieutenant. "But we solve most murders and arrest the killers. And we hope to dodge enough bullets to stay alive and collect our pensions."

They started to give me an informal third-degree. No rubber hoses or bright lights. Just the names of a few current murder movies they had seen—and hated. I hadn't written any of the films, but still I started to sweat—a kind of guilt-by-association feeling for the writers who did. Finally I confessed: Many Hollywood writers had gotten trapped in the excitement of their stories and had been careless with the truth. I promised to try to avoid that pitfall—and write an honest film about police detectives, if it ever got produced.

I started making the rounds of all the bureaus and offices of the police department concerned with homicide, picking up a little knowledge of law. Then I started to run into problems. My first obstacle was the elderly warden of the files, Inspector Joseph Donovan, who had a definite anti-Hollywood bias. He said he would cooperate with me but within the extent of the law, meaning that he would allow me to read the solved cases only. I explained that I could go to any newspaper morgue for the solved cases. It was the files of the unsolved cases that fascinated me—the anonymous tips to the police, statements of dying men. As he argued with me, I detected a touch of Brooklyn accent in his Irish brogue. I asked him what street he lived on in Brooklyn. Puzzled, he told me and I named the nearest cross streets. I then explained that I was from Brooklyn. His attitude softened as he called various police officials and said he had a lad from Brooklyn doing some research.

In the course of my wanderings, I learned that the Police Academy, then located in the Borough Hall district of Brooklyn, had a one-week refresher course for detectives. I wanted to sit in on the homicide courses, but was advised that no civilian was ever admitted. I finally tracked down Deputy Chief Cutrayne who was in charge of the Academy. He advised me that the Academy was none of my business. Besides, it was located on some tiny street in Brooklyn and I would never find it. As a native of Brooklyn, I recalled that the street was something like Pineapple Street, and I assured the Chief that I knew where Pineapple was. It was right next to similarly named streets—Lemon, Orange, etc. The indignant Chief was certain that I was making this all up, so I made a deal with him. If I was wrong, I would stop annoying him. If I was right, I would go to the Academy. We sent for a map of Brooklyn. I pointed to the area where I knew the Police Academy was located—and sure enough, there was a series of single-block streets—Pineapple, Lemon, Orange. The Chief OK'd a pass for me to go to the Academy. What he didn't know was that I had worked two years in the Brooklyn Post Office. I had memorized the Brooklyn City Scheme and knew the names and locations of every street in Brooklyn—a mass of trivia ingrained in my mind for many more years.

After my refresher course at the Police Academy, I watched the police at work questioning criminal suspects in the morning lineup, and I interviewed detectives from the homicide squad, which investigates all murders. I spent several uncomfortable hours at the city morgue watching the medical examiner and his assistants perform autopsies on recently arrived corpses. I sniffed lethal poisons in the test tubes of the city toxicologists. I peered at bullets through the double-barrelled comparison microscopes of the ballistic experts. I examined the spectrograph machines of the technical research laboratory. At the Bureau of Criminal Investigation, I met the "silent detectives," the files of criminal records. These records included the fingerprint files and the "rogues gallery," a file of criminal photographs categorized according to height and *modus operandi*.

When I returned to Hollywood, Hellinger demanded to know what story I had created out of all that research. I told him to his amazement that I had at least a dozen good stories. After all, there were eight million people in New York City, and, as Hellinger was later to say in final narration of the film, there are "eight million stories in the Naked City and this is just one of them."

Hellinger as a journalist had written about a thousand short stories for the Hearst press, and all of them had O. Henry endings, surprise twists. I knew that's what he wanted, and among the stories I told him was one about a beautiful blonde model, Dot King, who was found slain—her murder unsolved. I had seen some inside information in the files about this case, never revealed to the press, and I had a notion of how the crime might be theoretically solved—by using bits and pieces of other cases. Hellinger was excited because he had been in on that case. He and Winchell were riding with the police one night when the homicide call came. He had visited the murder apartment and had seen the corpse—and he had known the victim when she was alive.

"Write up an outline," Hellinger ordered, "but try and make the lead character a part that Jimmy Stewart can play." Mark and Jimmy had a gentlemen's agreement to work together some day. But as I sat down to my typewriter, a funny thing happened. Instead of a thirty-five-year-old detective, my leading character turned out to be a sixty-five-year-old veteran with an Irish brogue. Hellinger was annoyed. Where in the world would we find a sixty-five-year-old star? "Right here in Hollywood," I replied. "A recent Academy Award winner in *Going My Way*, Barry Fitzgerald." Hellinger was dubious. "We'll never get Fitzgerald for a crime picture—not after he just finished playing a priest."

But, being a long-shot player, Hellinger sent for Mr. Fitzgerald and his agent. "Mr. Fitzgerald, I know you are a busy man, but I have a young writer with the crazy idea that you might consent to play a detective in a script he wants to write."

"A detective?" Fitzgerald's bushy eyebrows shot up. "Why would you be thinkin' that I would want to play a detective?" Hellinger tossed me a gloomy look and indicated for me to answer the question. I reminded Fitzgerald that when he was a working actor in Dublin as a young man, many of his fellow-countrymen emigrated to New York and became cops. Some of them advanced to the ranks of detective, and a few became inspectors and deputy chiefs. Then I reeled off the names and ages of the department's top brass—and all were Irishmen of Mr. Fitzgerald's age.

He conceded that was a logical point, but then he asked, "Doesn't a detective do a lot of runnin' and shootin'?"

"Not necessarily," I replied. "His main job is investigation and interrogation, sitting across the desk from a suspect and trying to get at the truth in the criminal's black heart. And that's mostly talking."

Fitzgerald nodded thoughtfully. "Ah, that I could do," he agreed, "but I still want to know about the runnin' and the shootin'."

"For that," I explained, "we have a young detective, an actor like Don Taylor, who played Pinky in *Winged Victory*."

Fitzgerald meditated for a moment, then turned to Hellinger. "And when would you be shooting this film?"

Hellinger held his breath. "We were thinking about next summer."

Fitzgerald smiled. "Well, now," he said, "I think that would be lovely, seeing as how I would be free then. Mr. Hellinger, if you've a mind, you just got yourself an actor."

And with that the Irish Oscar-winner walked out of the room, with his agent trailing behind him. For a moment there was silence between Hellinger and me. Then he looked at me and grinned. "I'll be damned," was all he said.

It took me a week to complete an outline to Hellinger's satisfaction. But then, after reading it, doubts suddenly overwhelmed him about the entire project. At the time I was working for Hellinger, Richard Brooks was also employed by him as a writer on the screenplay of *Brute Force*. After Hellinger's death in 1948, Brooks wrote about Hellinger in *Screen Writer* magazine (March 1948):

> Mark lived in two distinct demi-worlds. In one world, he was secretive, suspicious, frantic, fearful. It was a world overwhelmed by jealous, greedy punks who were constantly trying to find a way to destroy him. Big executives were, he often complained, conniving against him, pulling off secret deals against him, planning to push him out of the movie business. Somebody or other was trying to grab all the glory away from him, make him appear a fool. He greeted each day as though catastrophe were about to befall him.

What concerned Hellinger was the way I wrote the outline in a bastard form—using the documentary-style presentation of a divided page with one half for the visuals, the other half for the narration, for the semi-documentary form. I then would resort to full-page treatment for the dramatic sections. The new form frightened Hellinger. He had never seen it before, but I explained it was common practice in the world of documentaries.

Then Hellinger revealed to me what he felt was a secret and made me swear I would never repeat it in his lifetime. "Look, pappy," he said, "I'm basically a writer, always will be. So when I assign a writer to a script, I become the collaborator. In other words I am the co-author. Now, here, you come along with a brand-new technique which I don't understand. So I can't possibly collaborate with you, as I do with my other writers. Therefore I can't have confidence in your script because I am not personally involved."

I was crushed. "All right," I asked, "what do you want to do—abandon the project?"

"No," he said slowly, "I love what you've written. I'm absolutely intrigued by the way you treat the city—the kind of romantic Walt-Whitman-type narration you're throwing in. I want you to do a treatment in this cockamamy style of yours—but I want you to know you're on your own. When the treatment is finished, if it's any good, I'll get Ben Hecht or John O'Hara to do the screenplay. That way you'll be guaranteed story credit at least." That was fine with me. From a few jokes in a column, I had parlayed my way into a screen treatment assignment.

When I finished the treatment, Hellinger sent for me and said, "Let's forget about Ben Hecht or John O'Hara. Hecht's from Chicago, O'Hara's from Pennsylvania. Do you think you can manage the New York scene all right in a first-draft screenplay by yourself?" I assured Hellinger I could. I was born in New York City, had gone to college in Brooklyn, did social work at a settlement house on the Lower East Side in the shadow of the Williamsburg Bridge (which was to be the setting for the spectacular chase at the end of the film), had been a reporter on a Brooklyn newspaper, and had been a Broadway song-plugger covering the radio stations, the jazz joints on 52nd Street, and the night clubs in Harlem.

I did the first draft and the second draft. By that time six months had elapsed since my first conversation with Hellinger. Hellinger sent for me one night at his mansion in Hollywood. His wife, the former Gladys Glad, once called "the most beautiful woman in show business," but now a fading beauty, seemed to stay clear of bright lights and walked in shadows. She left us alone, and Hellinger told me he had read my script, was fascinated by my semi-documentary approach but was worried about production problems. How can you shoot a film on the streets of New York and keep the crowds away? (I explained that the cops would exercise crowd control.) How about the proposed chase on the bridge? Autos used that bridge to get from Brooklyn to Manhattan. (Shut off that section of the bridge and use the lower section; besides, there were three other bridges spanning the East River.)

Finally, Hellinger confessed his real fear. He recalled to me that he had been a writer and then a staff producer under Jack L. Warner at Warner Brothers and produced such Humphrey Bogart successes as *The Roaring Twenties*, *They Drive By Night*, and *High Sierra*. He left Warner Brothers once to do an independent film at 20th Century-Fox with Jean Gabin and Ida Lupino. It was called *Moon Tide* and had artistic pretensions. But it was a flop, and when Warner took him back into his studio, he crowed that Hellinger was merely a staff man, couldn't do anything good on his own. Now Mark was on his own again with Mark Hellinger Productions at Universal-International Studios. His first film, Hemingway's *The Killers*, was out and seemed to be a hit. His next two films, both written by Richard Brooks, *Swell Guy* and *Brute Force*, were seemingly also destined for commercial success.

"Why," he asked me, "should I stick my neck out with experimental films when I'm doing so well in what I know best?"

"I'll tell you why," I replied. "Because at heart you're a gambler. You've gambled on horses, and you've gambled on cards. Why not really shoot for big stakes and gamble with your career?"

"But if I flop again," Hellinger protested, "Jack Warner will make me the laughingstock of Hollywood. He hates my guts, even though he says he's my pal."

"Mark," I said, "remember years ago when you wrote sketches for the Ziegfeld Follies, when Broadway musicals consisted of sketches and chorus girls kicking up their legs. Then along came Rodgers and Hammerstein, and they revolutionized musical theater with *Oklahoma*, which included a ballet scene. Well, ballet is like the documentary film, conceived by artists but later converted to commercialism."

I argued that Hellinger as a creative Hollywood producer could help advance the film world in a small way. But Hellinger protested that he was not in the business to experiment. How did I know that it would work out? My reply was that one producer—the New York based Louis de Rochmont—had already succeeded in 1945 with a semi-documentary called *The House on 92nd Street* shot mostly in New York City. In a month or so he would be out with a similar film, *13 Rue Madeline*, shot in Paris, and was planning *Boomerang* to be filmed in Connecticut. Thus there was ample precedent for going all out, turning the island of Manhattan into a film studio.

Hellinger shook his head. De Rochmont was famous as the man who made the *March of Time* semi-documentary shorts. He was a veteran, expert at shooting on location. Hellinger was a Hollywood studio man. He was adamant. He was not going to produce *The Naked City*.

(The original title of the film was "Homicide." Then one day, I chanced across a book of photographs called *The Naked City* by Weegee, a celebrated crime photographer. Hellinger bought the rights to the title for a thousand dollars, and this was to give rise to a whole series of subsequent titles with the word *naked* in it—such as *The Naked Prey* and *The Naked Jungle*. On the ridiculous side, a nudist colony in the midwest became famous as "The Naked City.")

Hellinger told me honestly that he had a half-dozen other scripts that he preferred to mine, all ready to go. Furthermore, he reminded me that he was an independent producer, doing his own financing. It was not wise for him to take risks; he had to play it safe with scripts that he was sure of. Sorry, Pappy, *The Naked City* was to go on the shelf—the fate of two out of every three scripts in studios.

I took a vacation and when I returned Hellinger called me. He had surprising news. He had changed his mind! He had given my script to his *Brute Force* director, Jules Dassin, who disagreed with Hellinger and thought there was a picture there, and it should be made. But what was needed was a final shooting script, and a top screenwriter to do it. Hellinger submitted the script to one of the best in Hollywood, Albert Maltz, famed short-story writer, playwright, and novelist and screenwriter of three of the finest films of that era—*This Gun for Hire, Destination Tokyo,* and *Pride of the Marines*. Much to Hellinger's delight, Maltz agreed to accept the assignment. Maltz's decision to do the script elated me, too. One moment I had been told the script was dead and now it was being brought back to life at the hands of an artist whose work I had long admired.

The finished result was what I had learned to expect from Maltz—

highly dramatic, exciting, preserving my original intent but bringing a fresh outlook and new shadings of plot and character.

During the summer of 1947 when the film was being shot in New York I heard all kinds of rumors. The police were not cooperating in holding off the crowds at the one hundred and seven locations. City bureaucrats were holding up production, and payoffs had to be made to cut red tape. Hellinger had suffered a heart attack. The film went about a half-million over budget. When Hellinger returned to Hollywood in the fall, I stayed away from him, figuring I was the cause of his trouble by selling him on the idea of shooting a film entirely on location. Then one day while visiting the studio, I was spotted by his secretary. She urged me to see Hellinger, who was wondering why I was avoiding him.

When I went to his office, I told him about the rumors I had heard and how much he had suffered making the film. Mark nodded soberly. He always wore a blue suit, a blue shirt, and a white tie, a kind of standard uniform reminiscent of the underworld figures he knew so well. He looked especially somber that day. "Yes," he said, "I suffered making that film. But you don't do anything great without suffering, and we have a great film here."

"Wonderful," I said with a sigh of relief. "I'm glad it turned out well. Do you think you can put me on the preview list so I can see it when it comes out?" Hellinger stared at me. "What do you mean— wait until the preview! You originated this thing—you with your cockamamy split-page, semi-documentary treatment. You're going to see the picture right now! I'm running it off for Howard Duff (who played a featured role in the film) and Ava Gardner."

I was thrilled with the work Dassin had done as a director on the film. After the showing, I went to congratulate him. There was one question I had for him. I recalled a scene in which the killer, Ted DeCorsia, is poised in flight on the Williamsburg Bridge and looks down—and there two hundred feet below can be seen people leisurely playing tennis in white clothing.

"Boy," I said, "you were lucky to have those people in white clothes playing below the bridge."

"Lucky," snorted Dassin indignantly, "I planted those tennis players there—they're extras! "

On December 16, 1947, Hellinger called me and swore me to secrecy. He was having a sneak preview of the film at the Loyola Theatre in Inglewood, California. I was to go there but tell nobody. My wife and I went and were dismayed that the audience laughed at some of the opening documentary scenes. "Don't worry," Hellinger told me the next day, "we'll cut some of those scenes. It will be all right."

According to the papers, on his way out of the theater, Hellinger had turned to Frank McFadden, his publicist, and said "That's my celluloid monument to New York. I loved it." In a way, *The Naked City* was to be a monument to Hellinger because less than a week later, while viewing the re-cut film at his home on a Saturday night, Hellinger had a heart attack, collapsed, and died the next day—at the age of forty-four.

Hellinger's friends in the press responded to his death, and the early reviews reflected it. *The Naked City* was heralded as an immediate hit. The *Hollywood Review* called it "A 4-Star Hellinger Monument"; the *Hollywood Reporter*, "A potent tale told with a master touch"; *Box Office Digest* referred to it as a "Smash Big Money Hellinger Hit." "Toweringly impressive," said *Hollywood Variety*. "A pulse-pounding thriller. It should come pretty close to paying off its negative cost on Broadway alone." New York *Variety* predicted that "It can't miss at the box office . . . The word of mouth . . . should be phenomenal."

The New York opening at the Capitol Theatre in March of 1948 was preceded by a barrage of raves from Hellinger's journalistic contemporaries: Walter Winchell, "One of the most thrilling moving pictures ever made"; Ed Sullivan, "Mayor O'Dwyer says it's the greatest picture ever written about New York City"; Quentin Reynolds, "The greatest motion picture Mark Hellinger ever made . . . I loved it." Most of the New York critics were equally enthusiastic. Whether it was because of the film technique or the recent death of the beloved Hellinger, the critics generally responded with superlatives.

I was delighted when Alton Cook commented in the *World-Telegram*: "The picture is about the most faithful version of actual police methods." That was what I had promised the police at headquarters, and I was glad to see that one critic felt it had been achieved. Howard Barnes in the *Herald Tribune* was more critical than his colleagues and assayed the script as "fairly honest" and characterized the film as a melodrama "which depends upon suspense for most of its impact." Archer Winsten in the *Post* was the only critic to pay special attention to the contribution of the director and the writers and their origins as New Yorkers. He called the film fascinating, rich with emotion and—

"very eloquent—very inside stuff." Bosley Crowther, the most distinguished of New York critics, complained in the *Times* that the subject matter was limited but praised the roaring "Hitchcock" end and assessed the film as a vivid job which came off as "spontaneous and unrehearsed."

The film boomed at the box office, grossing $1,600,000 in its first month of national release in April. *Consumers Union* in its national poll of critical evaluations determined that 70 percent of the film critics of America had rated the film excellent, 25 percent good, and only 5 percent fair—with an overall rating by the magazine of Excellent.

So much for the anatomy of a hit. But what happened to the creators? The producer had died. The director, Jules Dassin, soon found himself a political exile in the early days of McCarthyism and switched his career to Europe where his reputation as director of *The Naked City* preceded him. He achieved even greater fame as the director of *Rififi* in France and of *Never on Sunday*, *He Who Must Die*, and *Phaedre* in Greece. Albert Maltz and I were nominated by our peers for the first Writers Guild Award in two categories: best written American drama, and for the screenplay which deals most ably with problems of the American scene.

Photoplay magazine selected *The Naked City* as one of the ten best pictures of the year, and, as was the custom, invited the writers to attend the awards banquet. At the time of the awards Maltz, as one of the "Hollywood Ten," was on his way to a federal penitentiary for contempt of Congress during the House Un-American Activities hearings. The editors of *Photoplay* were embarrassed. They could not refuse to invite Maltz, but they saw to it that he and I were seated out of sight of the photographers, behind a palm tree, near the kitchen. That was nearly thirty years ago, and it was the first and last time I was to meet Albert Maltz. But as I recall it now, the rest of the banquet room was enthusiastically responding to the introductions of the stars who were being honored, and there sat Albert Maltz, one of America's most gifted writers, quietly sipping champagne, on his way to prison for defying Congress and pleading his First Amendment rights. If the scene were New York and not Hollywood, it could easily have been one of the "eight million stories of The Naked City."

In 1960, a dozen years after the release of the film, the following evaluation of *The Naked City* was made by Parker Tyler in his book *The Three Faces of the Film:*

The infiltraton of documentary into film fiction, whatever the artistic worth of its results, must be gauged as part of the overpowering forces of a technological era, in which film is still the important scientific discovery it once was hailed as. Scientific techniques, after all, have a secure and unchallenged place in modern social ethics. "The basic force behind documentary," to quote the historical statement of John Grierson, "was social not aesthetic." But there is another side to "the picture."

The hit film *Naked City* clearly showed that the documentary vogue in fiction had brought Grade B movies up to Grade A stature. This meant only one thing: the crime melodrama without star actors. In *Naked City* it is Manhattan Island and its streets and landmarks that are starred. The social body is thus, through architectural symbol, laid bare ("naked") as a neutral fact neither, so to speak, good nor bad, but something which, like the human organism itself, may catch a disease—the criminal—and this disease may elude its detectors. A good piece of intuition, in this light, was the incident near the end, the turning point, when the criminal in full flight bumps against a blind man and his seeing eye dog; the murderer's sadism flares, he fires his revolver at the annoying dog, and his pursuers are led to him by the report. In the same way the sick body blindly reacts to the hidden disease in it, and then draws the vigilant "police of the blood" to help fight the disease.

I don't think this analogy is a coincidence. The fact is that the vastly complex structure of a great city, in one sense, is a supreme obstacle to the police detectives at the same time that it provides tiny clues as important as certain obscure physical symptoms are to the trained eye of a doctor. As I have observed, the ideal of science dominates the fiction documentary in film, and the latter's technique is strictly analogous with the method of logical deduction (the abstract) as well as with the method of seeking out and following up clues (the concrete). Of course (and here the point presses against all the problems of true art), this film vogue is another modern means of avoiding the basic problems of the human spirit and of human society; in brief, it is a journalism of science as well as of fiction.

Editorial Note

The copy-text for this edition of *Naked City* is the mimeographed typescript dated 20 May 1947. Spelling, punctuation, and obvious typing errors have been corrected; and the camera directions have been regularized. Malvin Wald and Albert Maltz vetted the typescript. One substantive emendation was made in the dialogue by Mr. Maltz: 59. several people [several million people

Albert Maltz is a novelist and playwright as well as a screenplay writer. He received an Academy Award for his documentary film *Moscow Strikes Back*. Among his theatrical film credits are *Destination Tokyo*, *Pride of the Marines* and *Two Mules for Sister Sara*. He is the subject of a recent biography by Jack Salzman.

Malvin Wald teaches film writing at the University of Southern California. Twice a nominee for an Academy Award, he is a writer-producer for both the screen and television with such credits as *Outrage*, *Al Capone*, *Playhouse 90*, *Peter Gunn*, and *Daktari*.

Errata

Page iii, *For* By Malvin Wald and Albert Maltz *read* by Albert Maltz and Malvin Wald

Page v, *For* by Malvin Wald and Albert Maltz *read* by Albert Maltz and Malvin Wald

Page 1, *For* by Malvin Wald and Albert Maltz *read* by Albert Maltz and Malvin Wald

Page 2, *For* Screenplay by Malvin Wald and Albert Maltz, *read* Screenplay by Albert Maltz and Malvin Wald,